THE DEMANDS OF JUSTICE

THE DEMANDS
OF JUSTICE

James P. Sterba

UNIVERSITY OF NOTRE DAME PRESS
NOTRE DAME   LONDON

Copyright © 1980 by
University of Notre Dame Press
Notre Dame, Indiana 46556

Library of Congress Cataloging in Publication Data

Sterba, James P
  The demands of justice.

  Includes bibliographical references and index.
  1. Justice. I. Title.
JC578.S74   320'.01'1   80-10791
ISBN 0-268-00847-7

Manufactured in the United States of America

Contents

To
my mother and father,
who did so much more
than justice required

Acknowledgments

THIS BOOK HAS GROWN out of a series of projects undertaken over the last few years and supported in part by the Ludwig Vogelstein Foundation, the Earhart Foundation, and the University of Notre Dame. Earlier versions of most chapters, which have been considerably revised and augmented for inclusion in this book, were first presented at various American Philosophical Association meetings, at other philosophical meetings and conferences and a number of universities, and then later published as journal articles. An earlier version of Chapter 1 was published in the *Canadian Journal of Philosophy* (1979). Earlier versions of parts of Chapter 2 were published as "Justice as Desert" in *Social Theory and Practice* (1974) and as "Distributive Justice" in the *American Journal of Jurisprudence* (1977). An earlier version of Chapter 3 appeared as "Retributive Justice" in *Political Theory* (1977). Parts of Chapter 4 appeared as "Prescriptivism and Fairness" in *Philosophical Studies* (1976) and as "In Defense of Rawls against Arrow and Nozick" in *Philosophia* (1978). An earlier version of Chapter 5 appeared as "Neo-Libertarianism" in the *American Philosophical Quarterly* (1978), and part of Chapter 6 appeared as "Abortion, Distant Peoples and Future Generations" in *The Journal of Philosophy* (1980). I am grateful to the editors and publishers of these journals for permission to include some material from these articles.

Although I have incurred countless debts in writing this book, I wish in particular to thank Kurt Baier, James Buchanan, and Richard Wasserstrom for reading and commenting on the entire manuscript. I have also benefited from the written comments of John Rawls and R. M. Hare on parts of Chapter 4 and from some lively exchanges with Robert Nozick with respect to some of the arguments in Chapters 4 and 6. My deepest debt, however, is owed to my wife and fellow philosopher, Janet Kourany, who helped, encouraged, and disagreed with me to the very end.

Introduction

WHAT ARE THE DEMANDS of justice and why should one accept them? These questions have been the concern of philosophy from the very beginning for they are questions that virtually everyone has to face up to at some time or other.

Plato, for example, thought that justice demands the harmony of the soul and that, accordingly, being just best serves one's overall self-interest. Plato's view, however, never dispelled the widespread belief that, in an important sense, justice and self-interest can and do conflict.

Others, notably Immanuel Kant, took conflicts of justice and self-interest to be basic to human experience and sought to provide an alternative account of the demands of justice and why one should accept them. For Kant, the demands of justice are captured by those maxims that pass a certain test which he formulated in a number of ways. In one formulation, the test requires that a person act only on maxims that treat others as ends and never simply as means. In another formulation, the test requires that a person act only on maxims that one could legislate for "the universal kingdom of ends." But in the formulation which lends itself most readily to determinate application, the test requires that a person act only on maxims that he can will to be universal laws of nature. Applying this formulation of Kant's test, a maxim to steal whenever favorable opportunities arise cannot be a requirement of justice. This is because a person who wants to further his overall self-interest by stealing whenever favorable opportunities arise cannot consistently will such behavior to be a universal law of nature, since having *everyone* steal whenever favorable opportunities arise would conflict with the person's self-interest.

By taking conflicts of justice and self-interest to be basic to human experience, Kant's account of the demands of justice has attracted many defenders and thereby exerted considerable influence on contemporary ethical and political theory. Nevertheless, in at least two respects Kant's account is seriously defective.

First of all, Kant's favored formulation of his test for capturing the demands of justice, of "consistently willing a maxim to be a universal law of nature," will not serve to determine those demands. To understand why this is the case, consider the maxim not to steal whenever favorable opportunities arise. Surely this is the sort of maxim we would assume could be consistently willed to be a universal law of nature. But suppose a person wants to further his overall self-interest by stealing whenever favorable opportunities arise. Would it, then, not be inconsistent for such a person to will it to be a universal law of nature that *everyone* not steal whenever favorable opportunities arise? Obviously, willing this maxim to be a universal law of nature would conflict with the person's self-interest in just the same way that willing the maxim to steal whenever favorable opportunities arise to be a universal law of nature would conflict with the person's self-interest. In fact, whenever a question of justice is at issue, such conflicts will always be present, rendering it impossible for any maxim to be consistently willed to be a universal law of nature. Thus this formulation of Kant's test will not serve to determine the demands of justice. Nor is it clear how one would go about deriving determinate results from Kant's other formulations of his test.

Secondly, the only justification Kant provides for accepting the demands of justice is simply the stark assertion that they are required by reason. But without further elaboration to show why being unjust is unreasonable or irrational, such a justification is hardly designed to win over many to the banner of justice. What Kant in effect has done is create the expectation of a strong foundation for the demands of justice without providing that foundation. Thus it has been left to contemporary ethical theory to determine whether such an expectation can be justified.

This book attempts to remedy both of these defects in Kant's account by providing a determinate account of the demands of justice and indicating the best reasons available for accepting those demands.

Chapter 1 examines whether a justification for the demands of justice and morality can be provided by showing that ethical egoism is inconsistent, irrational, or somehow involves the denial of the reality of other persons. Various arguments are presented to show why such attempts to provide a justification for the demands of justice and morality are unsuccessful. The conclusion of the chapter is that a number of requirements, the most important of which is a requirement of fairness, must be accepted in order to provide an adequate foundation for the demands of justice.

The succeeding chapters of the book specify the demands of justice that are derivable from this requirement of fairness. In Chapter 2, the requirement is used to derive nonutilitarian principles of distributive justice that are significantly different from those John Rawls defends in *A Theory of Justice*. In Chapter 3 this same requirement is used to derive principles of retributive justice. Chapter 4 examines the major criticisms that R. M. Hare, Robert Nozick, and certain Marxists have directed at the general approach developed in Chapters 2 and 3. In Chapter 5, it is argued that virtually the same results which were defended in Chapter 2 can be justified by beginning with the libertarian's ideal of liberty. Chapter 6 explores how a requirement of fairness (and a right to life) can be used to support the welfare rights of distant peoples and future generations and considers the implications that accepting such welfare rights has for the liberal's defense of abortion on demand. Finally, Chapter 7 relates the overall results of the book to the descriptivist-prescriptivist debate in contemporary ethics and considers under what conditions the demands of justice may legitimately be overridden in the pursuit of other values.

While the conclusions of the book should be of interest to those who are working in moral and political philosophy, the arguments, as far as possible, have been developed in such a way as not to presuppose that the reader is familiar with the relevant literature. Hence the book should also be accessible to those who are just beginning to do philosophy. Of course, as with previous attempts to determine what are the demands of justice and why one should accept them, each reader should feel challenged either to accept the book's conclusions or to justify some alternative response to these perennial questions.

1. Ethical Egoism and Beyond

CONSIDER THE CASE OF Gary Gyges, an otherwise normal human being, who for reasons of personal gain has just embezzled $300,000 while working at People's National Bank and is in the process of escaping to the South Sea Islands, where he will have the good fortune to live a pleasant life, protected by the local authorities and untroubled by any qualms of conscience. If we assume that in the society from which Gyges is fleeing moral standards are generally observed, Gyges' behavior would be obviously immoral. Is it possible, however, that Gyges, a rational person, may have had perfectly consistent reasons for acting immorally? Is it also possible that Gyges may not have had any moral reasons at all to refrain from his act of embezzlement? To answer "yes" to the first question, that is, to hold that

    a)   a rational person may have perfectly consistent reasons for acting immorally

is to adopt a view which supports ethical egoism. To answer "yes" to the second question, that is, to hold that

    b)   a rational person may not have any moral reasons at all to refrain from acting immorally

is to adopt a seemingly more radical view that, until recently, has not had many defenders.[1]

    The above two views appear to be distinct, for it would seem that someone could accept (a) while consistently denying (b). But if (b) is false, with the consequence that a rational person always has at least some moral reasons for refraining from immoral actions, it can be argued that the overridingness of such reasons will be inconsistent with any reasons the person accepts as conclusive reasons for acting immorally, and hence (a) will also be false. Thus Gary Gyges would have had overriding moral reasons not to embezzle the money that were inconsistent with the self-interested reasons which he accepted as conclusive reasons for embezzling the money. Similarly, if (a) is false, it can be argued that (b) is as well, on the grounds that the falsity of (a) can only be explained by assuming that a rational person always has at least some moral reasons for refraining from acting immorally and that these reasons are inconsistent with any reasons the person accepts as conclusive reasons for acting immorally. Accordingly, Gary Gyges would have had inconsistent reasons for embezzling the money that are best explained by his having had some overriding moral reasons not to embezzle the money. Hence (a) and (b), in fact, mutually entail each other.

In this chapter I intend to provide sufficient grounds for accepting (a) and (b). In terms of our example, I hope to show that Gary Gyges' act of embezzlement may have been done for perfectly consistent reasons and that he may not have had any moral reasons at all to refrain from performing it. I shall also indicate what beliefs and commitments are necessary before a rational person can be said to have moral reasons for acting. I shall begin by distinguishing two forms of ethical egoism and then consider various arguments that purport to show that ethical egoism is inconsistent and, hence, that (a) is false.

Forms of Ethical Egoism

There are two forms of ethical egoism that should be distinguished:

> Individual Ethical Egoism: For every person X and every action y, X ought to do y if and only if y is in the overall self-interest of a particular person Z.

> Universal Ethical Egoism: For every person X and every action y, X ought to do y if and only if y is in the overall self-interest of X.

No doubt Individual Ethical Egoism is an extreme doctrine—imagine Gary Gyges claiming that everyone in the world ought to do what is in his overall self-interest. But what I want to consider is not the obvious practical deficiencies of this form of egoism but simply whether it is possible to coherently subscribe to it. Of course, one might object to calling either form of egoism an ethical theory. Individual Ethical Egoism seems particularly open to this objection because it bases all its directives on the interests of just one individual. But even Universal Ethical Egoism, which *does* take into account everyone's interests, can be criticized on the grounds that its directives cannot be publicly advocated. For when a Universal Ethical Egoist's interests are at stake it would rarely be in his overall self-interest to tell others what he really believes they ought to do. These objections, however, are more plainly directed at the inappropriateness of regarding either form of egoism as a moral theory, where that implies that certain criteria of fairness have been met. While "ethical" seems to be free from such implications, the reader who still feels uneasy with "ethical" should substitute "normative," "rational," or "practical" throughout, so as not to lose sight of the central issue of whether egoism in either of these forms can be coherently defended.

Universal Ethical Egoism

To show that some form of egoism is a coherent view, it is necessary to interpret and justify its use of "ought" in such a way that no inconsistencies result. At first glance, this would seem to be impossible to do in the case of Universal Ethical Egoism, the view most often defended by philosophers. Thus suppose (to refer again to our earlier example) that Hedda Hawkeye, a fellow employee of Gary Gyges at People's National Bank, knows that Gyges has been embezzling money from the bank and now plans to escape. Suppose, further, that to prevent Gyges from escaping with the embezzled money is in her overall self-interest, since she will be generously rewarded for doing so by being appointed vice-president of the bank. Granting that it is in Gyges' overall self-interest to escape with the embezzled money, it now appears that we can derive a contradiction from the following:

1) Gyges ought, all things considered, to escape with the embezzled money.

2) Hawkeye ought, all things considered, to prevent Gyges from escaping with the embezzled money.

3) Hawkeye's preventing Gyges from escaping with the embezzled money = Hawkeye's preventing Gyges from doing what he ought, all things considered, to do.

4) One ought never prevent someone from doing what he ought, all things considered, to do.

5) Therefore, Hawkeye ought not, all things considered, to prevent Gyges from escaping with the embezzled money.

Since (2) and (5) are contradictory, it has been claimed that Universal Ethical Egoism is inconsistent.

The soundness of the above argument depends crucially, however, on premise (4), and the defender of Universal Ethical Egoism believes there are grounds for rejecting (4). For if by "preventing an action" one means "rendering the action impossible," it would appear that there *are* cases in which a person is justified in preventing someone else from doing what he ought, all things considered, to do.[2] Consider, for example, the following case. Suppose that Irma and Igor are actively competing for the same teaching position at a prestigious university and that each would benefit from the appointment. If Irma is offered the position and accepts, she obviously renders it impossible for Igor to be appointed to that position. But surely this is not the kind of prevention we would intuitively think ought not to be done. Nor would Hawkeye's prevention of Gyges' escape appear to be an unacceptable form of prevention. Thus, to sustain the above argument against Universal Ethical Egoism, one must distinguish between acceptable and unacceptable forms of prevention, and then show that the argument goes through for forms of prevention that a Universal Ethical Egoist would regard as unacceptable. This requires getting clear about the force of "ought" in Universal Ethical Egoism.

To illustrate the sense in which a Universal Ethical Egoist claims that other persons ought to do what is in their overall self-interest, defenders of this form of egoism have often appealed to an analogy with competitive games. Thus, for example, in baseball a catcher might believe that the runner on first base ought to try to steal second base, while not wanting him to do so and even being prepared to try to stop him if he tries. Again, to use Jesse Kalin's example,

> I may see how my chess opponent can put my king in check. This is how he ought to move. But believing that he ought to move his bishop and check my king does not commit me to wanting him to do that, nor to persuading him to do so. What I ought to do is sit there quietly, hoping he does not move as he ought.[3]

The point of these examples is to suggest that a Universal Ethical Egoist may, like a player in a game, judge that others ought to do what is in their overall self-interest, at the same time that he attempts to prevent such actions or at least refrains from encouraging them.

The analogy with competitive games can also illustrate the sense in which a Universal Ethical Egoist claims that he himself ought to do what is in his overall self-interest. For just as a player's judgment that he ought to make a particular move is followed, other things being equal, by an attempt to perform the appropriate action, so, likewise, when a Universal Ethical Egoist judges that he ought to do some particular action, other things being equal, an attempt to perform the appropriate action follows. In general, the defender of Universal Ethical Egoism would want to stress that since we have little difficulty understanding the asymmetrical implications of the use of "ought" in competitive games, we should have little difficulty understanding the analogous asymmetrical implications of the use of "ought" by the Universal Ethical Egoist.[4]

However, it is not clear that interpreting the "ought" of Universal Ethical Egoism as analogous to the "ought" of competitive games is sufficient to protect this view from the charge of inconsistency. For in the examples cited, one's opponent is always granted at least the right to try to make the appropriate move, whether it be stealing a base or putting one's king in check. Such a right presupposes that certain preventive actions, like intentionally blocking a player trying to steal or changing the positions of chess pieces while one's opponent is distracted, are not permitted. But by refraining from such preventive actions, a person could lose the game, and, as the analogy with competitive games is being employed, the counterpart to losing the game for the Universal Ethical Egoist is not acting in his overall self-interest. Hence if the analogy with competitive games is intended to apply strictly, a Univeral Ethical Egoist would be committed to refraining from performing certain types of preventive actions and, as a consequence, would fail to act in his overall self-interest. But this would entail a contradiction, since the Universal Ethical Egoist would then be required to refrain from doing what he could not be required to refrain from doing.

Another way to put this criticism of Universal Ethical Egoism is to claim that the theory violates the principle that an action-guiding "ought" implies "can." According to this principle, plausibly interpreted, saying that Herman ought, all things considered, to go into business for himself implies that it is within his power to do so, which is to say that doing so is either directly or indirectly under his voluntary control.[5] According to Universal Ethical Egoism, on the other hand, saying that Herman ought, all things considered, to go into business for himself is perfectly compatible with saying that Hilda (whose interests conflict, all things considered, with Herman's) will actually prevent Herman from even attempting to go into business for himself (e.g., by robbing him of everything he owns). Hence the apparent inconsistency of Universal Ethical Egoism can be said to be reflected in a violation of the principle that an action-guiding "ought" implies "can," with the result that the theory appears to be unable (in Kurt Baier's words) "to coordinate the activities of those whose activities it is designed to direct."[6]

Yet it is possible that these unacceptable results are derivable only because egoism is being defended in a universal form and that consistency can be preserved by subscribing to Individual Ethical Egoism. It is that possibility that I now want to explore.

Individual Ethical Egoism

In Individual Ethical Egoism, all directives are based on the overall interests of just one particular individual. Let us call that individual Seymour. Because Seymour's interests constitute the sole basis for determining directives in Individual Ethical Egoism, it would seem that the problem of inconsistent directives that plagued Universal Ethical Egoism will not arise—assuming, of course, that it is possible to harmoniously integrate Seymour's particular interests. The crucial problem for Individual Ethical Egoism, however, is providing a justification for allowing only Seymour's interests to count in determining directives. While the justification need not provide conclusive or even good reasons for accepting Individual Ethical Egoism, at least it must be possible to provide some reason for basing all directives exclusively on the interests of Seymour rather than basing them exclusively on the interests of Raul or Stanislaus or some other individual (for these are surely competing possibilities). Otherwise, acceptance of Individual Ethical Egoism would border on the irrational.

But what reason or reasons could serve this function? Clearly, it will not do to cite as a reason some characteristic that Seymour shares with other persons, for, whatever justification such a characteristic would provide for favoring Seymour's interests, it would also provide for favoring the interests of those other persons. Nor will it do to cite as a reason some characteristic of Seymour that only he happens to have, like knowing all of Hegel's writings by heart, for such a characteristic involves a comparative element, and consequently others with similar characteristics, like knowing some or most of the Hegelian corpus by heart, would still have some justification, although a proportionally lesser justification, for having their interests favored. But then the proposed characteristic would not serve to justify favoring only the interests of Seymour.

A similar objection could be raised if a unique relational characteristic were proposed as a reason for Seymour's special status—like Seymour's being the husband of Samantha. Since other persons would have similar though not identical relational characteristics, similar though not identical reasons would hold for them. Nor will it do to argue that it is not the particular unique traits that Seymour possesses that provide a reason for Seymour's special status, but rather the mere fact that he has traits that are characterized by uniqueness. For the same would hold true of everyone else. They too have traits that are characterized by uniqueness. And if recourse to unique characteristics is dropped, and Seymour simply claims that the reason for his special status is that he is himself and wants to further his own interests, every other person could claim the same, since it is true of each person that he is himself and wants to further his own interests.[7]

If the Individual Ethical Egoist were to argue that the same or similar reasons do *not* hold for other persons who have characteristics that are the same or similar to those of Seymour, then, to be consistent, he must provide an explanation of why they do not hold. It must always be possible to understand how a characteristic serves as a reason in one case but not in another. If no explanation can be provided, and certainly in the case of Individual Ethical Egoism none has been forthcoming, then the proposed characteristic either serves as a reason in both cases or it does not serve as a reason at all.

We have therefore reached a serious impasse. Neither form of egoism would appear to be open to a consistent defense. Nor does it appear possible—given the generality of the objections that have been raised to each form of egoism—to formulate some other version of egoism that would not be open to at least some of these objections. If egoism is to survive as a normative theory, therefore, one or more of the objections that have been raised against it must be defused.

The Consistency of Universal Ethical Egoism

Now any attempt to defend Individual Ethical Egoism against its objections would require universalizing the theory to allow for an appeal to reasons to support its directives. This universalization would not necessarily yield Universal Ethical Egoism, however. For the revised theory could base its directives on the interests of some particular group of persons, though it would then no longer be an egoistic theory. It would seem, therefore, that any defense of *egoism* must provide an answer to the objections raised against Universal Ethical Egoism—must provide, that is, some interpretation of the Universal Ethical Egoist's use of "ought" that does not lead to inconsistent results.

Actually, the defender of Universal Ethical Egoism has a choice, since there are two interpretations of "ought" that can free the theory from the charge of inconsistency, and, surprisingly, each interpretation, allowing for some differences, parallels a use of "ought" in standard moralities. To understand what these uses of "ought" are, imagine that for each person in society we determine a range of life plans specifying what is in the person's overall self-interest under various possible circumstances. Suppose we order the life plans for each person so as to correspond to the degree to which the life plans assume the cooperation or noninterference of other persons with respect to what contributes to the person's overall self-interest. Thus for each person, life plan$_1$ assumes the full cooperation of other persons with respect to what contributes to the person's overall self-interest. Gary Gyges' life plan$_1$, for example, assumes the full cooperation of Hedda Hawkeye, the bank officials, and others with respect to what contributes to his overall self-interest, and Hedda Hawkeye's life plan$_1$ assumes the full cooperation of Gary Gyges, the bank officials, and others with respect to what contributes to her overall self-interest. And similarly for other persons. Life plans of a somewhat lower order assume that other persons at least do not interfere with respect to what contributes to the overall self-interest of the person concerned, and life plans of a still lower order assume varying degrees of interference by other persons.

Given that people's interests conflict, many persons would find it impossible to cooperate fully with respect to what contributes to the overall self-interest of others without sacrificing their own overall self-interest to some degree. Hence it would be impossible for everyone in society to jointly realize his life $plan_1$.

If we were to claim, therefore, that Universal Ethical Egoism requires that

  I) each person ought, all things considered, to realize
    his life $plan_1$

we would have the option of either maintaining, as critics have, that (I) has direct action-guiding implications or else denying that (I) has any direct action-guiding implications at all.

If we maintain that (I) has direct action-guiding implications, then the action-guiding implications of (I) can be directly inferred from the description of each person's life $plan_1$. Thus the action-guiding implications for Gary Gyges would be that he should do his part, according to his life $plan_1$, assuming the full cooperation of Hawkeye, the bank officials, and others with respect to what contributes to his overall self-interest. And the action-guiding implications for Hedda Hawkeye would be that she should do her part, according to her life $plan_1$, assuming the full cooperation of Gyges, the bank officials, and others with respect to what contributes to her overall self-interest. However, in our example, and in society, if we maintain that (I) has direct action-guiding implications, then these implications would be inconsistent since it is not possible for Gyges and Hawkeye, as well as for everyone in society, to jointly realize his or her life $plan_1$. Furthermore, these action-guiding implications would also violate the principle that an action-guiding "ought" implies "can," for everyone would not be able to do what he or she ought to do according to these action-guiding implications.

By contrast, if we maintain that (I) does not have direct

action-guiding implications, then the action-guiding implications of (I) cannot be directly inferred from the description of
each person's life plan$_1$ but, rather, depend on which actions a
person is able to perform in the circumstances in which he
finds himself. Accordingly, the action-guiding implications
for Gyges would be that he ought, all things considered, to
escape with the embezzled money only if he is able to do so in
the circumstances in which he finds himself. Hence if we
maintain that (I) does not have direct action-guiding implications, then the action-guiding implications for Gyges and
Hawkeye, as well as for everyone in society, would not be
inconsistent, nor would they violate the principle that an
action-guiding "ought" implies "can," for everyone would
always be able to do what he or she ought to do according to
these action-guiding implications. Of course, maintaining that
(I) does not have direct action-guiding implications is a rather
unusual way to interpret a conclusive "ought," but, as we
shall see, it does parallel a use of "ought" in standard
moralities at the same time that it successfully avoids the
charge of inconsistency.

Inconsistency can also be avoided by appealing to yet
another interpretation of the Universal Ethical Egoist's use of
"ought." That is, instead of claiming that each person ought,
all things considered, to realize his life plan$_1$, one might claim
that

II)   each person ought, all things considered, to realize
        the highest-order life plan he is able to realize in the
        circumstances in which he finds himself.

Since the circumstances in which a person finds himself normally involve varying degrees of cooperation and interference
by others with respect to what contributes to that person's
overall self-interest, it would normally be impossible for anyone to realize his or her life plan$_1$. Under most circumstances,
persons would only be able to realize life plans of various
lower orders. Interpreting the Universal Ethical Egoist's use of

"ought" in this way would have direct action-guiding implications because each person would always be able to do what he or she ought, all things considered, to do. Thus Gary Gyges would be able to escape with the embezzled money if that is what he ought, all things considered, to do according to interpretation (II). Under this interpretation, therefore, there would be no conflict between what each person ought, all things considered, to do. Thus the problem of inconsistent directives simply would not arise, nor would there be any violation of the principle that an action-guiding "ought" implies "can."

Interpretations (I) and (II) not only free Universal Ethical Egoism of the charge of inconsistency, they also parallel similar uses of "ought" in standard moralities. Imagine that we are again determining life plans for persons in society, but this time we specify a range of life plans for each person on the basis of what he would have to do to meet the requirements that a standard morality would place upon him under various possible circumstances (any standard morality will do as an example). We then order the life plans for each person in a way that corresponds to the degree to which the particular life plan assumes that other persons will fulfill the requirements this standard morality places upon them. Thus each person's plan$_{m1}$ assumes that other persons will completely fulfill the requirements this standard morality places upon them, while life plans of lower orders assume correspondingly lesser degrees of fulfillment.

Now while, as we have noted, it is not possible, if people's interests conflict, for everyone to jointly realize his life plan$_1$, it *is* possible, under conditions of conflicting interests, for everyone to jointly realize his life plan$_{m1}$. This constitutes an important difference between these two types of life plans.[8] Nevertheless, if we further assume that some people will seriously neglect the requirements that this standard morality places upon them, then not everyone else will be able to realize his or her particular life plan$_{m1}$. For example, if someone robs me of everything I own, I will be unable to meet at least some of the obligations I have to care for my family under my life plan$_{m1}$, and if the government decides to unjustly imprison me for the rest of my life, there will be many obligations under my life plan$_{m1}$ that I will be unable to meet.

If we were to claim, therefore, that this standard morality requires that

I_m)   each person ought, all things considered, to realize his life plan$_{m1}$,

we would have the option of maintaining either that (I_m) has direct action-guiding implications or that it does not.

If we maintain that (I_m) does not have direct action-guiding implications, then we are employing a use of "ought" that parallels interpretation (I), proposed for Universal Ethical Egoism. Accordingly, this interpretation would have consistent action-guiding implications and would not violate the principle that an action-guiding "ought" implies "can."

By contrast, maintaining that (I_m) has direct action-guiding implications would lead to inconsistent results. The inconsistent results in this case would not be due to any inconsistency in the action-guiding implications of (I_m) for ideal conditions, in which everyone lived according to them, but would be due to the fact that, for nonideal conditions in which some people significantly depart from these implications, the action-guiding implications of (I_m) would violate, while presupposing, the principle that an action-guiding "ought" implies "can." For under the proposed interpretation it would be perfectly legitimate to say that Herman ought, all things considered, to realize his life plan$_{m1}$, even when Hilda will, in the course of disregarding her own life plan$_{m1}$, actually prevent Herman from doing what he ought, all things considered, to do—for instance, by robbing him of everything he owns. This violation of the principle that an action-guiding "ought" implies "can," therefore, would clearly be inconsistent with maintaining that the proposed interpretation of "ought" has direct action-guiding implications.[9]

There is, of course, a consistent interpretation of "ought" with direct action-guiding implications that is used by standard moralities. According to this interpretation,

II_m) Each person ought, all things considered, to realize the highest-order life plan$_m$ he is able to realize in the circumstances in which he finds himself.

Since the circumstances in which a person finds himself normally involve varying degrees of fulfillment by others of the requirements placed upon them by this standard morality, it will normally be impossible for everyone to realize his or her life plan$_{m1}$. Rather, some persons will only be able to realize life plans of various lower orders. The main advantage of this use of "ought" in standard moralities is that it has direct action-guiding implications that are compatible with the principle that an action-guiding "ought" implies "can." This use of "ought" also parallels interpretation (II), proposed for Universal Ethical Egoism.

If we now apply each of the proposed interpretations of "ought" to our original example of Gyges' embezzling, we get the following results. According to interpretation (I), Gyges ought to escape with the embezzled money, and Hawkeye ought to prevent Gyges from escaping. But since these ought-claims have no direct action-guiding implications, their requirements can be met by Gyges' and Hawkeye's undertaking any number of different actions. For example, depending on the circumstances, the directive that applies to Hawkeye can be met by Hawkeye's actually preventing Gyges from escaping, or by her unsuccessful attempt to do so, or by her recommendation of a better accounting system to prevent future embezzlements, etc. Thus the action-guiding implications of such a directive would depend on what actions Hawkeye is able to perform in the circumstances in which she finds herself and on the overall purpose of the directive. In this case, the overall purpose of the directive is to increase the benefits Hawkeye derives from her employment. According to interpretation (II), however, Gyges ought to escape with the embezzled money only if he is able to do so. But if he is able to do so, then, under interpretation (II), it is not the case that Hawkeye ought to prevent Gyges from escaping with the money. Given these circumstances, probably what Hawkeye ought to do, all things considered, is gain the favor of the bank officials by recommending a better accounting system to prevent future embezzlements.

Thus interpretations (I) and (II) can be used by the Universal Ethical Egoist to express consistent directives. Yet, even if we grant this, we might still question, as we did in the case of Individual Ethical Egoism, whether this form of egoism can be consistently justified. Here we are not asking the Universal Ethical Egoist to provide a good or conclusive reason, but only some reason or other, in support of his position.

But suppose, in response, the Universal Ethical Egoist claims that the justification he has for adopting his position is that he is himself and wants to further his own interests. How, then, can we fault him for inconsistency, since, unlike the Individual Ethical Egoist, he is willing to universalize that claim and recognize that everyone else has the same justification for adopting Universal Ethical Egoism? We would seem to have no recourse but to grant that the Universal Ethical Egoist can provide a consistent justification for his position.

Nevertheless, the consistency of Universal Ethical Egoism might still be challenged on the grounds that no rational person could restrict himself to using only the two interpretations of "ought" that are available to the egoist. Indeed, one might claim that a rational person must employ some standard moral interpretation of "ought," such as (I_m) or (II_m), or at least the "ought" of competitive games, which implies a commitment to a principle of fair play. Now if a

rational person is required to assent to any of these senses of
"ought," it would be inconsistent for him to follow the directives of Universal Ethical Egoism in cases where there is conflict of interest. For in such cases the directives of Universal
Ethical Egoism would violate various principles of standard
moralities, including a principle of fair play. But what justification is there for claiming that a rational person must endorse
some sense of "ought" other than those available to the Universal Ethical Egoist?

In support of this view, it might be argued that there are
certain goods, such as freedom and well-being, that a rational
person would want to lay claim to by using a sense of "ought"
that has stronger implications concerning the noninterference
of others than those senses available to the Universal Ethical
Egoist.[10] Thus, while (II) implies that others cannot or will not
interfere with a person's doing what he ought to do, (II_m)
carries the additional implication that others ought not to interfere with a person's doing what he ought to do. Similarly,
while neither (I) nor (I_m) implies that others cannot or will not
interfere with a person's doing what he ought to do, (I_m), like
(II_m), implies that others ought not to interfere with a person's
doing what he ought to do. Hence (I_m) and (II_m) carry a
stronger implication concerning the noninterference of others
than do their respective counterparts, (I) and (II). By using (I_m)
or (II_m), a rational person, in claiming he ought to have a
certain share of freedom and well-being, would imply that
others ought not to deprive him of that share. The justification
a rational person would have for wanting to lay claim to freedom and well-being by using a sense of "ought" that carries
this stronger implication is that these goods are necessary for
the performance of all voluntary actions. Given the importance
of these necessary goods for voluntary action, it is understand-
able that a rational person might want to lay claim to them,
using a sense of "ought" so strong that it renders inconsistent
his prevention of others from acquiring a similar share of these

goods for themselves. Yet the important question remains, whether a rational person *must* commit himself to such a strong sense of "ought."

Publicly, no doubt, a rational person would want to assent to institutions that give expression to a moral sense of "ought," such as (I_m) or (II_m), in order to prevent others from interfering with what is in his overall self-interest. Yet, since that assent could be sheer hypocrisy, the crucial question is whether a rational person must *sincerely* commit himself to such institutions. After all, why can a rational person not judge that his overall self-interest is better served if, instead, he sincerely, albeit privately, commits himself to the directives of Universal Ethical Egoism? Suppose that, privately, he also thinks that others ought to commit themselves to those same directives, while publicly he condemns them whenever it becomes evident that they are so committed. There are times, then, when he thinks that others ought to perform actions that would interfere with his most basic freedom and well-being. Yet because he and others publicly endorse institutions that prohibit, and attempt to punish, any interference with a person's most basic freedom and well-being, and since a good many people are in fact sincerely committed to such institutions as well, he is normally able to escape such harm to himself. There are also times when he is able to further his overall self-interest by interfering selectively, and usually secretively, with the most basic freedom and well-being of others, and privately he judges that he ought to perform such actions, and often he does. He is careful, however, that he does not seriously undermine those institutions he privately violates. In this way a person surely may be able to secure for himself a greater share of the necessary goods of freedom and well-being than he would if he privately committed himself to the institutions he publicly endorses, for in the world as we know it, injustice and immorality *do* have their days of triumph. Hence the concern a rational person has for the necessary goods of freedom and well-being need *not* require him to sincerely assent to a stronger sense of "ought" than those senses that are available to the Universal Ethical Egoist.

A Universal Ethical Egoist can thus provide a consistent interpretation and justification of his use of "ought" that a rational person can accept; so it follows that

    a)   a rational person may have perfectly consistent reasons for acting immorally

and, consequently,

    b)   a rational person may not have any moral reasons at all to refrain from acting immorally

are true. Since most of us are not Universal Ethical Egoists (or at least so it seems), it must be in virtue of some commitment we have made that a rational person can consistently reject. What needs to be determined, therefore, is the minimal commitment a person would have to make, after which it would be inconsistent for him to accept the directives of Universal Ethical Egoism. If this minimal commitment is all but practically inescapable, virtually everyone would have reason to go beyond Universal Ethical Egoism.

Ethical Egoism and Solipsism

Getting beyond Universal Ethical Egoism would present no challenge at all if, as has been recently argued by Thomas Nagel, the consistent egoist is actually a type of solipsist: one who denies the reality of other persons.[11] The basis for traditional solipsism is the belief that first- and third-person psychological judgments are radically different, that in fact they share no common meaning. According to this view, to say "I am in pain" and to say of someone else "Manfred is in pain" is to make two quite different judgments: the first expresses a private psychological condition, the second can be construed as a behavioristic report. Because these judgments are construed to be radically different by the solipsist, third-person judgments are not understood to provide evidence for the existence of other persons or other minds.[12]

What the consistent egoist is thought to share with the traditional solipsist is an analogous bifurcation of meaning between first- and third-person uses of "ought." Thus, it is claimed, when the consistent egoist says "I ought, all things considered, not to steal Oscar's wife," he means something radically different from when he says of someone else, "Hugo ought, all things considered, not to steal Oscar's wife." The former judgment is said to have motivational content, which the latter judgment lacks. By contrast, third-person uses of "ought" are said to have motivational content for the non-egoist; that is to say, they imply that the person who makes a judgment at least wants the relevant ends to be attained (e.g., Hugo's not stealing Oscar's wife), yet without necessarily being committed to any specific action. Because the consistent egoist's first- and third-person uses of "ought" are so radically different in content, Nagel claims, the consistent egoist, like the traditional solipsist, in fact denies the reality of other persons. The consistent egoist's use of "ought" is said to prevent him from conceiving of himself as a person among others who are equally real.

Obviously, if this argument were correct, merely sincerely affirming the equal reality of other persons would suffice to render inconsistent one's commitment to Universal Ethical Egoism. Virtually every rational person, therefore, would have reason to go beyond egoism. It is far from clear, however, that making a radical distinction between first- and third-person uses of "ought" is sufficient to commit the consistent egoist to a position analogous to traditional solipsism; but even supposing that this were so, the consistent egoist would still not be a solipsist, since he can avoid making this distinction.

To understand how this is possible, we must look carefully at the way in which Nagel believes the nonegoist is motivated by third-person ought-judgments. Suppose the nonegoist judges that

1) Franklin ought to have a two-bedroom apartment and
2) Olga ought to have a new car.

According to Nagel's account, by sincerely making these ought-judgments, the nonegoist is not thereby motivated to provide Franklin with a two-bedroom apartment or Olga with a new car. For the most part, he is initially motivated only to want Franklin to have a two-bedroom apartment and to want Olga to have a new car. What specific actions result from these wants will depend on various factors. If our nonegoist is in no position to procure a two-bedroom apartment or a new car, he will be motivated simply not to interfere with attempts by Franklin or Olga to acquire these goods. But if the nonegoist is in a position to procure or help procure these goods, then, assuming that he knows of no conflicting interests, the nonegoist would be motivated to do what he can to help. Yet if, as is probable, the nonegoist knows that securing a two-bedroom apartment for Franklin or a new car for Olga would conflict with pursuing other interests, he would have to employ some principle to decide which interests to pursue. Various principles, of course, have been proposed for resolving conflicts of interest, such as the maximin principle, which favors the least advantaged, and the total and average principles of utility. What specific actions a nonegoist is motivated to perform in cases of conflict of interest will depend, therefore, on what particular principle he accepts for resolving these conflicts.

Now the consistent egoist's position can be viewed as strictly analogous to that of the nonegoist. He too can be motivated to want Franklin to have a two-bedroom apartment and to want Olga to have a new car, and if, perchance, he knows of no conflicting interests, he can also be motivated to

do what he can to help. Nevertheless, if he is aware of conflicting interests, as will almost always be the case, the egoist's
principle for resolving such conflicts is clear:

> Promote the interests of others only when they are a
> means to realizing one's own overall self-interest or
> when they are not inconsistent with that pursuit.

It follows that the egoist can allow the interests of others to
count, but never to take precedence over his own interests.
Thus the egoist need not differ from the nonegoist with respect
to whether third-person uses of "ought" have motivational
force. He can grant that they do. Where he differs from the
nonegoist is with regard to the principle he uses for resolving
interpersonal conflicts of interest.[13]

To go beyond Universal Ethical Egoism, therefore,
clearly requires a commitment to some principle for resolving
interpersonal conflicts of interest which is inconsistent with the
directives of Universal Ethical Egoism. This would require
commitment to some principle for resolving interpersonal conflicts of interest that at least sometimes requires the person to
sacrifice his overall self-interest to benefit the interests of others. One version of such a principle would restrict the amount
of harm a person could do to another in pursuit of his overall
self-interest. Another would restrict a person's pursuit of his
overall self-interest to the degree necessary to secure for others
the satisfaction of certain basic needs and interests. And of
course there are other possibilities. What we want to know,
therefore, is how to render a person's commitment to go beyond Universal Ethical Egoism as rationally defensible as possible.

From Egoism to Fairness

Let us begin by determining the minimal requirement that
must be imposed on normative theories in order to rule out

commitment to Universal Ethical Egoism. A strong candidate for such a requirement is a more defensible version of the Kantian requirement of universalizability (discussed in the Introduction). This requirement can be stated as follows.

> *The Universalizability Requirement:* It must be possible for the directives of a normative theory to be universally followed, and such a possibility must be acceptable to those who are committed to the theory.

Now consider how a Universal Ethical Egoist would react to this requirement. Obviously, he would not be anxious to have everyone follow the directives of the normative theory to which he is committed. Still, everyone *could* follow the directives of Universal Ethical Egoism under either interpretation (I) or (II), and a Universal Ethical Egoist should "accept" such a possibility in the sense that he should recognize, at least in private, that he cannot legitimately protest such egoistic behavior on the part of others. Nevertheless, a Universal Ethical Egoist should not "accept" such a possibility, in the sense that he would refrain from actively opposing such egoistic behavior on the part of others. This is because a Universal Ethical Egoist would be decidedly less successful at furthering his own interests when others are also following the directives of Universal Ethical Egoism. Moreover, it is probable that his interests would be better served by everyone's (including himself) following the directives of morality rather than the directives of Universal Ethical Egoism.[14] Consequently, the practice of Universal Ethical Egoism by others would certainly tend to undercut the justification a Universal Ethical Egoist would have for following the directive of his normative theory in the first place. On that account, a Universal Ethical Egoist would have good reason actively to oppose the practice. Consequently, if an acceptance that rules out active opposition is demanded by the Universalizability Requirement (and this seems to be the appropriate interpretation), Universal Ethical Egoism would not be able to meet the requirement.[15]

This shows that Universal Ethical Egoism is not a normative theory for all times and places. A person's justification for
following the directives of Universal Ethical Egoism clearly
depends on a sufficient number of other persons not following
those same directives. By contrast, a person's justification for
following the directives of morality clearly depends, at least in
many cases, on a sufficient number of other persons' following
those same directives (e.g., a moral directive to pay one's
taxes). There are, however, other normative strategies that
resemble Universal Ethical Egoism in this respect. For example, when a person goes through an educational program that is
designed to prepare him for a particular profession (say that of
a college teacher), many other persons may do the same,
thereby effectively destroying the person's chance for employment in that profession. Accordingly, a person's justification for going through such a program may also depend on a
sufficient number of other persons' not doing the same. Of
course, the Universal Ethical Egoist (unlike many would-be
college teachers) is usually willing to take strong measures to
prevent others from acting as he does. Nevertheless, when he
fails to achieve this result and other persons *do* take up the
practice of Universal Ethical Egoism, his justification for
being an egoist tends to be undercut. Consequently, to impose
the Universalizability Requirement and thus require that a
normative theory not have its justification undercut by its general practice would effectively exclude commitment to Universal Ethical Egoism.

Unfortunately, while excluding commitment to Universal
Ethical Egoism, the Universalizability Requirement does not
suffice to exclude commitment to many grossly immoral normative theories, for the Universalizability Requirement only
demands that the universal practice of a particular normative
theory be acceptable to persons who are committed to that
theory. It does not demand that the universal practice of the
normative theory be acceptable to persons who are not com-

mitted to the theory but are nevertheless forced to adhere to its directives. As a result, the requirement does not exclude, for example, commitment to normative theories which are based on race or slavery, for those who belong to the "superior" race, or are slaveholders, may well have good reason to favor universal adherence to the particular normative theory to which they are committed. Of course, the ill treatment of "inferior" races and slaves may render a social order unstable and thus make revolution more likely. Nevertheless, this may not always be the case, and even when it is, those who benefit from the practice of the particular normative theory may rightly judge that the benefits that accrue to them are well worth the risks. Hence to rule out commitment to such grossly immoral normative theories, some further requirement is needed. A requirement that obviously suggests itself is the following.

> *The Requirement of Universal Acceptability:* The directives of a normative theory must be acceptable to everyone who would be affected by them if the theory were universally followed.

This requirement goes a long way toward ruling out the grossly immoral normative theories that could satisfy the Universalizability Requirement, for it rules out all those immoral normative theories that would not be acceptable to persons who would be extremely disadvantaged under them, that is, persons who would have good reason actively to oppose the practice of such theories. Nevertheless, it is possible for universal adherence to the directives of a particular normative theory to be acceptable to everyone, even when those directives are radically unfair. This is because those who are unfairly treated under a particular normative theory may still have good reason not actively to oppose the directives of that theory. For example, it may be well known that such opposition would lead to modifications in the prevailing theory that would be even more unfair. Under these circumstances, universal adherence to the directives of a particular normative theory would still be relatively stable. It is certainly arguable that many existing societies are based on just such a radically unfair compromise.

What we need to do at this point, then, is impose a Fairness Requirement on normative theories. But how should we characterize such a requirement? It seems clear that a Fairness Requirement applies primarily to activities in which persons compete for scarce or limited social goods, like money or victory in a game. What fairness ideally requires in such contexts is that the competitive activity be conducted according to rules that would be freely accepted by rational persons who are aware of both the possibilities for structuring the activity and the degree of interest each has in engaging in the activity. Since the persons choosing the terms of the competition are aware of the amount of interest each has in engaging in the competitive activity, it would be impossible for any of them to gain a special advantage by claiming to be less interested than, in fact, he or she is. Nor would an agreement be *freely* arrived at if some, but not others, were pressured into reaching that agreement in order to satisfy their basic needs.

Yet in practice the rules of competitive activities only approach this ideal. Frequently the rules of competitive activities heavily favor persons who have minimally developed certain prized native abilities, such as strength or good looks, or persons who already have considerable social goods over those who have developed as best they can their more limited native abilities and social goods. Nevertheless, so long as the rules of the competitive activities are not radically unfair and the stakes are not too high, engaging in such activities can still provide each person with considerable enjoyment and benefit. And when those who are not favored in such competitions are able to beat the odds and do well, their enjoyment and benefit can be quite intense. Yet when the stakes are high, it is more important, to at least some of the participants, that the rules of the activity satisfy a Fairness Requirement.

Clearly, when the stakes of a competition are high, a Fairness Requirement generally is no longer being applied to small-scale competitive activities like games and contests. Rather, it is being applied to competitive activities involved in the most fundamental distribution of social goods in society, that is, the distribution of social goods that are necessary for the satisfaction of each person's basic needs. It is at this point that a Fairness Requirement becomes equivalent to a Justice Requirement and we have the ideal of "justice as fairness." Of course, it is not easy to comprehend what rules or principles would be freely accepted by rational persons who are aware of both the possibilities for structuring the fundamental competitive activities of a social system and the amount of interest each of them has in engaging in those activities. It may be that only when the ideal is expressed as it is in succeeding chapters does it lend itself to clear application.

Yet, even assuming that a Fairness Requirement can be adequately characterized and applied, the question remains: How should fairness be morally weighed in conflicts with such other values as utility, human perfection, and high culture? Fortunately, this problem is not as serious as it might appear. First of all, it can be argued that although fairness can be legitimately sacrificed to other values in certain contexts, nevertheless, when we are dealing with fairness as it applies to the most fundamental distribution of social goods in society— that is, when we are dealing with justice as fairness—we are dealing with a fundamental moral value that is rarely, if ever, to be sacrificed to other values. (This would explain, for example, why utilitarians have generally restricted themselves to showing that the ideal of justice as fairness *does not conflict* with maximizing utility.) Secondly, even in contexts in which initially it seems plausible to claim that other values morally outweigh the value of justice as fairness—for example, when the competing values are those of human perfection or high culture—it can be argued that the plausibility of such a claim diminishes once the implications of justice as fairness are better understood. When better understood, justice as fairness will often be seen as an all but indispensable means in the pursuit of other values.

To say all this, however, is not to deny that justice as fairness may still be morally outweighed by other values in certain contexts. It is only to claim that once the ideal of justice as fairness is better understood, both by contractarians, who generally take justice as fairness to be a fundamental moral value, and by utilitarians and perfectionists, who generally accept justice as fairness as a fundamental moral value but then take some other value to be more fundamental, the possibility that justice as fairness may be morally outweighed by other values will not appear to be a recurrent practical problem.

If this line of reasoning is accepted (and obviously its acceptability depends in large part on how the ideal of justice as fairness is developed in succeeding chapters), then to go beyond Universal Ethical Egoism and embrace an adequate moral theory not only requires commitment to the Universalizability Requirement and the Universal Acceptability Requirement but also requires commitment to the Fairness Requirement, which will be developed in the following chapters.

2. Distributive Justice

SOCIETIES ARE RARELY, if ever, what they ought to be when judged from a moral point of view. To some degree this is the result of the failure of societies properly to educate their members to the requirements of morality or to follow up that education with the system of moral and legal sanctions that is necessary for the proper enforcement of those requirements. Somewhat more frequently, this failure of societies to measure up to the requirements of morality is due to the willful violation of those requirements by both individuals and whole social classes. But to some degree this failure can also be attributed to the fact that the requirements themselves have not been clearly perceived or sufficiently articulated even by moral philosophers, who would normally be expected to have some expertise in the matter. As a result, many people can claim in good conscience that they are committed to ideals of justice and social welfare while, at the same time, endorsing particular actions that are inconsistent with those ideals. What is needed, therefore, is a clear and straightforward deduction, indicating what particular policies and actions are required by commonly accepted moral ideals. In this chapter an attempt will be made to meet this need in the case of the commonly accepted ideal of justice as fairness. This same ideal has been discussed in some detail by John Rawls in *A Theory of Justice*. Since this ideal is commonly accepted, it is certainly important to understand exactly what commitment to the ideal entails. What I hope to show in this chapter is that this ideal of justice as fairness requires principles of distributive justice that are significantly different from the principles Rawls defends.

Rawls' Decision Procedure

In *A Theory of Justice*, John Rawls attempts to draw out the implications of this commonly accepted ideal of justice as fairness by fashioning a decision procedure from which only principles that accord with this ideal can be chosen.[1] To understand the nature of this procedure, imagine that we are trying to determine what would be fair principles for governing the relationships between workers, employers, government officials, and the general public—that is, every member of society insofar as he or she has an interest in our social and economic system. We might begin (assuming it were practically possible) by having a general meeting of representatives of all the relevant interests. Such a meeting, if each representative were given a chance to argue in favor of his or her particular interest, might result in greater appreciation for all the relevant viewpoints; however, it would be unrealistic to think that a meeting of this sort would necessarily result in the selection of fair principles for governing relationships among all the represented parties. The chances of that occurring would be very slight, unless there were some way to conduct deliberations at the meeting so that each relevant interest received its "proper weight" from a moral point of view. For if fair decisions are to be reached, the method of reaching decisions must go beyond the number of individuals supporting each interest to take into account the relative importance of majority and minority interests.

In *A Theory of Justice*, John Rawls uses a decision procedure that employs an "ignorance condition" to guarantee fair decisions among persons with conflicting interests. For example, if a judge were to attempt to arbitrate a case fairly in which his nephew was one of the plaintiffs, the fact that his nephew was one of the plaintiffs could not be one of the reasons for his decision in the case; that is, the judge would have to discount his prejudicial interest in his nephew in making his decision. Now being ignorant or imagining oneself to be ignorant of prejudicial interests of this sort is simply another method of satisfying the demands of fairness when attempting to arrive at decisions in conflict-of-interest situations. Fairness requires that persons discount prejudicial interests in arbitrating conflict-of-interest situations, and imagining oneself to be ignorant of those prejudicial interests has the same effect. Indeed, fairness requires that persons discount all their special interests, including their particular conception of the good, when consideration of these special interests would preclude unanimous hypothetical agreement in conflict-of-interest situations. Accordingly, a person's special interest in his own social position, talents, sex, race, and religion all must be discounted in order to fairly arbitrate situations where his special interests conflict with the interests of others, and, as before, imagining oneself to be ignorant of all these special interests has the same effect.

Suppose, then, we were to employ this decision procedure at the meeting where all who have an interest in our social and economic system are represented. Each person at the meeting would attempt to reach a decision about the principles he favors for governing the social and economic system while imagining himself to be ignorant of his or her special interests. Employers, for example, would imagine themselves ignorant of the fact that they are employers and would attempt to decide what principles they would find acceptable, assuming it were possible that they might in fact turn out to occupy any of the relevant positions having an interest in the social and economic system. Other representatives at the meeting would employ the same method of discounting their own special interests. Given the availability of information for assessing each of the represented interests and the ability of each of the parties to rationally assess that information, this method of decision making would culminate in a unanimous decision. This is because each representative would be deliberating in a rationally correct manner with respect to the same information and would be using a decision procedure leading to a uniform evaluation of the alternatives; consequently, all would favor the same principles for governing their social and economic system.

The Argument for Rawls' Principles

Rawls maintains that persons using this decision procedure would choose the following two principles of distributive justice:

1) Each person is to have an equal right to the most extensive total system of equal basic liberties compatible with a similar system of liberty for all.

2a) Social and economic inequalities are to be arranged so that they are to the greatest benefit of the least advantaged and (2b) are attached to offices and positions open to all under conditions of fair equality of opportunity.

Rawls claims that the first principle would be taken to have priority over the second whenever the liberties guaranteed by the first principle can be effectively exercised by persons in all social positions. This means that when this condition is satisfied, liberties are not to be sacrificed for the sake of obtaining increased shares of other social goods. For example, it would not be considered just for a society to give up freedom of the press in order to achieve greater economic benefits. But when the liberties guaranteed by the first principle cannot be effectively exercised by persons in all social positions, Rawls argues that persons using his decision procedure would favor the following, more general conception of justice:

> All social values—liberty and opportunity, income and wealth and the bases of self-respect—are to be distributed equally unless an unequal distribution of any, or all, of these values is to the advantage of the least favored.

Rawls also holds that a priority would be assigned between the two parts of the second principle, that 2b would be given priority over 2a, whenever the opportunities guaranteed by 2b can be effectively exercised by persons in all social positions. Thus, when this condition is satisfied, it likewise would be considered unjust to sacrifice basic opportunities to attain larger shares of economic goods. Similarly, Rawls allows that when this condition is not satisfied, persons using his decision procedure would be willing to dispense with this priority in favor of the more general conception of justice. According to Rawls, for societies that can satisfy the conditions for effective exercise of basic liberties and opportunities, it is these two principles, with their priority rules, that would be chosen by persons employing his decision procedure.

Rawls believes these two principles would be chosen because the choice situation that is defined by his decision procedure, which he calls the "original position," is a situation in which the maximin rule for choice under uncertainty applies. Since the maximin rule assumes that the best one can do is maximize the payoff to the least advantaged position, the principles that would be chosen by persons in the original position are considered to be the same as those a rational person would choose for the design of a society in which his enemy would assign him his position, which, of course, would be the least advantaged position. This is not to say that persons in the original position believe that their place in society is so determined, because then their reasoning would be based on false premises, and Rawls finds that unacceptable. Still, the principles that persons would select in both situations would be the same, according to Rawls, because both situations are such that the maximin rule for choice under uncertainty applies.

Rawls argues that the original position possesses, to a striking degree, the three features that make a choice situation appropriate for applying the maximin strategy. Those features are:

1. There is some reason to discount the probabilities that are arrived at in the choice situation.
2. The person choosing has a conception of the good such that he cares very little, if anything, for what he might gain above the minimum he can in fact be sure of gaining by following the maximin strategy.
3. Alternative strategies have outcomes that the person choosing can hardly accept.

According to Rawls, the first feature is characteristic of the original position because persons in the original position would not have any objective grounds for assigning probabilities to their turning up in different positions in society, and it would not be reasonable for persons so situated to rely on any probability assignments in the absence of such grounds. In addition, Rawls argues that since persons using his decision procedure would want their choice of principles (and strategies) to seem reasonable to others, particularly their descendants, they would have still another reason for not relying on probability assignments that would be made in the absence of objective grounds.

Yet, contrary to what Rawls claims, persons in the original position would have objective grounds for assigning probabilities. Those grounds would be provided by the general and particular facts that Rawls' decision procedure allows to be taken into account in the choice of principles of distributive justice. More specifically, persons in the original position have unrestricted general information about themselves and their society. They also know that they are contemporaries, that they are in circumstances in which cooperation is both possible and desirable, and that they are each capable of abiding by the principles they select. Consequently, judging from the objective basis provided by the facts which are known to them in the original position, persons so situated might well be tempted to conclude that, since they have no reason to think they in fact occupy one position in society rather than another, it is reasonable to suppose that it is equally probable that they occupy each of the positions in their society.

Nevertheless, Rawls may ultimately only want to claim that the objective grounds that are available to persons in the original position are simply not sufficient grounds on which to support such a conclusion. This would certainly be a plausible stance for Rawls to take. For given the importance of the choice of principles to persons in the original position, it would appear reasonable for them to require stronger grounds before concluding that it is equally probable that they occupy each of the positions in their society. Moreover, this is all that is needed to show that the original position has the first feature that is characteristic of situations where it is appropriate to apply the maximin strategy.

In discussing the second feature, Rawls begins by arguing that his two principles of justice would guarantee a satisfactory minimum. He then goes on to claim that if the priority of liberty (and presumably the priority of opportunity) could be established in the original position, persons so situated would have no desire to try for greater gains at the expense of equal liberties (or opportunities) and that, consequently, they would be content with the minimum provided by the maximin strategy. Now it is only this second consideration which is relevant to determining whether persons in the original position care very little, if anything, for what they might gain over and above what they can gain by following the maximin strategy. The fact that Rawls' two principles of justice would guarantee a certain minimum has no bearing on this issue. What is of concern is whether the original position possesses to a high degree one of those features which is characteristic of situations where it is appropriate to apply the maximin strategy. The fact that Rawls' principles of justice would guarantee a certain minimum would only be relevant once it has been determined what strategy would be adopted by persons in the original position, since the overall aim of Rawls' argument was to show that the choice of the maximin strategy in the original position would lead to the choice of his two principles of justice, and not that the choice of his two principles would lead to the choice of the maximin strategy. In any case, Rawls fails to show that the original position possesses the second feature that is characteristic of situations where it is appropriate to apply the maximin strategy. Even holding that certain priority rules would be acceptable in the original position does not commit persons so situated to the choice of the maximin strategy. Persons in the original position could accept the priority of liberty and opportunity and, at the same time, maintain that the maximin strategy does not provide an acceptable distribution of primary economic goods. Certainly it does not seem correct to say, as the second feature requires, that, with respect to primary economic goods, persons so situated would care very little, if anything, for what they might gain if they were to support a lower minimum than what is required by the maximin strategy. Repeatedly, Rawls claims that persons in the original position would ordinarily want more, rather than fewer, primary social goods.[2] Presumably, then, they would be interested in supporting a suitable minimum that is lower than that required by the maximin strategy if they could thereby secure greater opportunity to acquire such goods. Thus it is far from clear that persons in the original position are restricted to those minimal desires which are characteristic of choice situations where it is appropriate to apply the maximin strategy.

To show that the original possesses the third feature that characterizes situations where the maximin strategy is said to apply, Rawls merely notes that, without priority rules, the principles of total and average utility, under certain conditions, might lead to serious infractions of liberty and that, consequently, the strategies which would lead to these principles would be unacceptable.³ But obviously, something similar holds true for the principles which are justified by the maximin strategy. Without priority rules, the maximin strategy might often justify the sacrifice of liberty and opportunity for the sake of greater economic benefit. On the other hand, if the principles of total and average utility were similarly restricted by rules giving priority to liberty and opportunity, many of Rawls' objections to these conceptions of justice would cease to apply. Of course, Rawls could reply that such "mixed" conceptions of justice do not appear on the list of alternatives from which persons in the original position are said to make their choice. Now, while these mixed conceptions *are* excluded, apparently for reasons of simplicity, it should also be noted that, for some unapparent reason, Rawls' own conception of justice, involving general and special principles of justice, does not appear on the list of alternatives either.⁴ Only his special principles of justice are listed as an alternative. At best, therefore, the list is a rough guide to the sorts of alternative conceptions of justice that persons in the original position can be expected to have considered.

In any case, I hope to provide principles of distributive justice that would be preferred by persons in the original position, both to Rawls' conception and to any alternative conception that persons so situated can reasonably be expected to have considered. In this way, it will also become apparent that the original position lacks the third feature which is characteristic of situations where it is appropriate to apply the maximin strategy.

The Choice of a Strategy in the Original Position

It is difficult to characterize the strategy which persons in the original position would employ in choosing principles of distributive justice. Possibly the best way of characterizing the appropriate strategy is to show what specific principles would be chosen by persons in the original position and then characterize the strategy in retrospect. Once it has been determined what principles of distributive justice would be chosen, it should be much easier to grasp the nature of the strategy which is implicit in the choice of those principles. In any case, this is the procedure I will adopt for characterizing the appropriate strategy for the original position.

In deciding what principles of distributive justice they should adopt for their society, persons in the original position would have to take into account the various social and economic conditions that could realistically arise in their society. For example, suppose that a considerable number of those occupying the least advantaged position in their society have freely opted to remain at that position.[5] These individuals *could* rise to more advantaged positions, but they have chosen not to do so because their basic needs are already more than satisfied and because they have other needs and interests that they would rather pursue. Accordingly, these individuals do not consider the larger shares of primary social goods, attached to more advantaged positions, worth the contribution demanded by society from anyone who occupies those positions. Suppose also that, unlike the members of this group, the other members of the society have chosen positions requiring contributions to society that correspond with their natural abilities. Let us suppose, that is, that we are faced with conditions similar to those that appear to obtain in many technologically advanced societies.

Now consider two possible principles that persons in the original position could adopt to govern the distribution of additional primary social goods for these circumstances. One principle would distribute additional primary social goods, resulting from increased productivity, primarily according to a person's contribution to society. The other principle would give members who have increased their productivity only what would be necessary to sustain their incentive to contribute to society, while siphoning off as large a portion as possible for the benefit of the least advantaged. Suppose that the adoption of either principle would produce exactly the same increase in productivity among the members of this society, although both principles would leave the productivity of those occupying the least advantaged position unchanged. Which principle, then, would persons in the original position find more reasonable to adopt for such a society?

Surely if the persons in the original position were rationally committed to the maximin strategy, they would favor the second principle, which allocates as large a share as possible to the least advantaged. But would it not be more rational for them to adopt the first principle, given that the least advantaged already have their basic needs more than satisfied and that a considerable number of those who occupy that position have freely decided not to improve their situation by contributing to their society? Moreover, the first principle still allows for the distribution of some of the additional primary social goods to the least advantaged, although it does not require, as the second principle does, that this group be given as much as the other members of the society will tolerate before they begin to contribute less.

The above example is simply a special case of a more general type of situation in which individuals who occupy various positions in society have chosen not to rise to more advantaged positions in order to avoid the greater contribution to society that would be demanded from them at those positions. Since the maximin strategy, after requiring that the welfare of the least advantaged representative person be maximized, would require the maximization of the welfare of the second least-advantaged person, and so on, coming at last to the most advantaged person and requiring the maximization of his or her welfare, it should be apparent that the choice between distributing primary social goods primarily according to a person's contribution beyond what is necessary to maintain incentive, as opposed to distributing these goods so as to satisfy the maximin strategy, applies in a special way to each and every representative position. Moreover, the more advantaged the representative position, the stronger the argument for distributing primary social goods on the basis of a person's contribution to society rather than according to the maximin strategy.

Consideration of realistic possibilities such as these would, I contend, have considerable impact on persons in the original position. In particular, it would lead them to be very careful of the way in which they specify the minimum for their society. Clearly, they would want an acceptable minimum of primary social goods to be guaranteed to each person in their society. The desirability of requiring an acceptable minimum from the point of view of the original position is beyond dispute. Persons in the original position do not know what positions they occupy in their society, nor do they know what natural or acquired traits or skills they have. Once the veil of ignorance is lifted, they may turn out to be the least talented person in the least advantaged position. Consequently, in their choice of principles of distributive justice they would surely want to guard against that possibility.

Of course, persons in the original position would realize that, because of limited social or economic resources or for reasons of incentive, it may be impossible to provide each person in their society with a minimum of primary social goods, irrespective of whether those who are capable make at least a minimal contribution to their society. Under such circumstances, it would be reasonable for persons in the original position to require from those who are capable at least that minimal contribution which is necessary to provide everyone with an acceptable minimum. Possibly, circumstances could be so adverse that only those members of society who have made their maximal contribution to society could be provided with even a minimum. Now there are at least two ways of dealing with such a possibility: either deny that in fact such circumstances do arise in just societies, or admit that at times they do obtain, and that when they do, a more generalized hypothetical choice situation, in which the parties behind the veil of ignorance are representatives of different societies, would require that the condition be remedied through contributions from those societies that have greater social and economic resources.

Suppose, however, there are sufficient social and economic resources, and the incentive to contribute to society would not be adversely affected if a minimum of primary social goods were guaranteed to each person, without requiring any contribution to society from those who are capable of contributing. For such conditions to obtain, of course, most of those who are capable of contributing to society must be willing to do so in excess of any minimal contribution that could possibly be required of them. In addition, presumably a certain level of prosperity must have been attained in a society so that the incentive of those contributing to society would not be adversely affected by the fact that some members of their society would be receiving a minimum of primary social goods without having made even the minimal contribution of which they are capable. But the question is whether, given these favorable conditions, persons in the original position would choose to require a minimal contribution to society from those who are capable of contributing.

Certainly, if such a contribution were required, there would be more primary social goods to distribute to those who are making more than the minimal contribution to their society. But the desire of persons in the original position for greater rather than smaller shares of primary social goods must be weighed against their desire to secure a minimum of primary social goods as a means to realizing whatever conception of the good life they happen to have. For example, some may be carrying out a life plan which would be very difficult to realize unless they were provided with a minimum of primary social goods, irrespective of whether they made any contribution to society. Consequently, under favorable conditions, where there are sufficient social and economic resources and where the incentive to contribute to society would not be adversely affected, persons in the original position would choose to provide each person in their society with a minimum of primary social goods, irrespective of whether the person made any contribution to society; that is, unless it could be shown that realizing the person's conception of the good life does not conflict with making a minimal contribution to society.

Nevertheless, even though persons in the original position would want, under favorable conditions, to guarantee a certain minimum to each person in their society, irrespective of whether they made any contribution to society, they would object to maintaining the highest possible minimum that would not adversely affect the incentive of those who are contributing to their society. They would realize that there may be a significantly large number of individuals in their society—call them Free Riders—who are so satisfied with a lower minimum (e.g., one specified in terms of the satisfaction of basic needs) that, although these Free Riders can attain additional social goods in return for making some contribution to their society, they choose instead to pursue other needs and interests. While the Free Riders are refusing to contribute to society to receive additional primary social goods, other members of society— call them Hard Toilers—may be contributing as much as they can to society in order to receive their highest attainable share of primary social goods. On this account, persons in the original position would object to providing the highest possible minimum that would not adversely affect incentive as required by the maximin strategy. Now it is important to understand why persons in the original position would take this stand.

Obviously, persons in the original position must specify

what minimum they want, in ignorance of whether they tend to be found among the Hard Toilers or the Free Riders. It may in fact be the case that they will function differently at different times in their lives. Since persons in the original position are ignorant of their particular propensities, they would certainly do best to assume that ordinarily they would want more rather than fewer primary social goods. This is a reasonable assumption, since if in fact they receive more than they want, they can easily give away the excess. Otherwise, they can be content that they did their best in the original position to satisfy their desires for such goods. The reason for the qualification ''ordinarily'' is that persons in the original position would want to secure for themselves an acceptable minimum even if this decreased their overall expectations to some degree. Subject to the constraint of an acceptable minimum, however, persons in the original position would seek to arrange the distribution of primary social goods on the assumption that they want more rather than fewer primary social goods. Consequently, in the particular circumstances being considered, they would assume that whether they tend to be found among the Hard Toilers or the Free Riders, they can still be said to want a larger rather than a smaller share of primary social goods.

However, assuming that contributing to society has the same disutility for both Free Riders and Hard Toilers, there would be a difference in the strength of their presumed desires for larger shares of primary social goods. Although the Free Riders can be assumed to want more rather than fewer primary social goods (as they were characterized), they do not want more than a certain minimal share of such goods strongly enough to contribute to their society in order to receive a larger share. Nonetheless, they would tend to favor any way of raising their share of primary social goods as long as it did not involve a contribution on their part to society. The Hard Toilers, however, can be presumed to want primary social goods in a stronger sense, since they in fact are contributing to society in order to receive more than the minimal share. They may in fact be contributing as much as they can in order to receive the largest share of primary social goods that they can attain in their society. In any case, unlike the Free Riders, they want more than the minimal share, enough to contribute to their society in order to get more.

Since primary social goods are relatively scarce in society, the highest possible minimum could only be maintained by restricting the shares of primary social goods to the Hard Toilers, whose contributions to their society evidence the stronger desires for those goods. If the Free Riders are to have larger shares of primary social goods, the Hard Toilers must have smaller shares. Thus persons in the original position would be faced with a choice, the nature of which can be illustrated by the example on the following page.

Under the conditions of the example, if the maximin strategy were chosen by persons in the original position, then Hard Toilers would presumably acquire an additional utility payoff of 10 units by choosing to make an additional contribution to society, and Free Riders would presumably acquire an additional utility payoff of 15 units by choosing to pursue their other needs and interests. On the other hand, if the alternative strategy were chosen, the Hard Toilers would presumably acquire an additional utility payoff of 12 units by choosing to make an additional contribution to society, and Free Riders would be faced with the choice of whether to acquire an additional utility payoff of 15 units by choosing to make an (additional) contribution to society or to acquire an additional utility payoff of 13 units by choosing to pursue their other needs and interests. Now for these circumstances, persons in the original position would choose to favor the Hard Toilers over the Free Riders, thus selecting the alternative strategy over the maximin strategy, for the following reasons.

First of all, if the alternative strategy were chosen, the Free Riders would be able to compensate themselves for their loss of utility simply by making a contribution to society, whereas if the maximin strategy were chosen, the Hard Toilers may not be able to do the same for themselves. From the point

	Hard Toilers		Free Riders	
	Maximin Strategy	*Alternative Strategy*	*Maximin Strategy*	*Alternative Strategy*
Disutility of (Additional) Contribution to Society*	−5	−5	−5	−5
Utility of Primary Social Goods Attainable by Contributing to Society	+15	+17	+15	+18
Utility of (Additional) Primary Social Goods Attainable without Contributing to Society	does not apply		+4	+2
Utility of the Pursuit of Other Needs and Interests	+5	+5	+11	+11
Payoff with (Additional) Contribution to Society	+10	+12	+14	+15
Payoff without (Additional) Contribution to Society	+5	+5	+15	+13

*Utilities and disutilities are assumed to have cardinal interpersonal significance.

of view of the original position, therefore, it would be rational
to specify the minimum so that those who receive less than
they might otherwise receive, and are presumably dissatisfied
as a result, would be able to compensate themselves for their
lesser shares and their presumed dissatisfaction, if they were to
choose to do so.

Secondly, if the alternative strategy were chosen, the
Hard Toilers would not be required to support the Free Riders
at a greater loss to themselves when the Free Riders could
achieve the same level of benefit for themselves if they so
desired.

Thirdly, persons in the original position could not discount the conflict between Free Riders and Hard Toilers as
unrealistic. For it would be unrealistic to assume that everyone
in society would always be willing to support themselves by
contributing to society, even when they could derive just the
same or more benefit by relying on the contribution of others.

Of course, the highest possible minimum required by the
maximin strategy could be implemented in a society and then
persuasion, education, and coercion could be used to motivate
Free Riders to support themselves by contributing to society,
rather than by relying primarily on the contributions of others.
But the cost of such a program and the resulting loss of liberty
to the Free Riders, together with the above considerations,
would surely favor the selection of a minimum similar to that
required by the alternative strategy. For these reasons, therefore, even under favorable conditions, where there are sufficient social and economic resources and incentive would not
be adversely affected, persons in the original position would
still not select the highest possible minimum, as required by
the maximin strategy.

Principles of Distributive Justice

But what minimum would persons in the original position
choose? One possibility is that they would specify the

minimum indirectly by choosing to maximize their average expected utility in society. John Harsanyi and others have argued that this is the only possible choice that could be made by persons using Rawls' decision procedure.[6] Harsanyi claims that persons in the original position would first assign an equal probability to their occupying each particular position in society and then select the social arrangement with the highest average expected utility. To determine utility assignments, persons in the original position are said to compare what it would be like to have particular distributive shares in society while possessing the subjective tastes of persons who have those shares. Similar comparisons are required by R. M. Hare's universalizability criterion, by Hume's impartial spectator, and by the Golden Rule. Harsanyi assumes that with knowledge of the appropriate psychological laws and factual information, persons in the original position would arrive at the same comparative utility judgments, from which it would then be possible to determine which social arrangement maximizes their average expected utility.

For example, consider a society where the members are equally divided between the Privileged Rich and the Alienated Poor. Suppose that persons in the original position assign the following utility values to two alternative social arrangements for this society.

	Social Arrangement A	Social Arrangement B
Privileged Rich	55	40
Alienated Poor	10	20

Given these alternatives, Harsanyi thinks that persons in the original position would assume it was equally probable that they would belong to each group and, therefore, would select Social Arrangement A as having the higher average expected utility. And if the utility values for the two alternative social arrangements were the following,

	Social Arrangement A'	Social Arrangement B'
Privileged Rich	50	40
Alienated Poor	10	20

Harsanyi thinks that persons in the original position would be indifferent between the alternatives.

According to Harsanyi, any risk aversion that persons in the original position might have in evaluating alternative social arrangements would be reflected in a declining marginal utility for money and other social goods. Thus, in our example, we could imagine that a yearly income of $100,000 may be required to provide each of the Privileged Rich with a utility of 55 while only a yearly income of $5,000 may be required to provide each of the Alienated Poor with a utility of 10. Similarly, a $60,000 yearly income may suffice for a utility of 40 and a $15,000 yearly income for a utility of 20.

But even if we assume that declining marginal utility of social goods has been taken into account, might not persons in the original position still have grounds for preferring Social Arrangement B to Social Arrangement A? To the person in the original position, might not the chance of having a utility of 55, rather than 40, be insufficient to offset the equal chance of having a utility of only 10 rather than 20? Or, at least, might not persons in the original position prefer Social Arrangement B' to Social Arrangement A'? Consider that, in the original position, persons are imagined to be selecting, once and for all, among different social arrangements. If they select Social Arrangement A', and their chosen arrangement is fully complied with, then each person would definitely have either a utility of 50 or a utility of 10. There would be no reason for them to expect that there would be a grand lottery every year or so, giving each person an equal chance to be either among the Privileged Rich or among the Alienated Poor. As a result, the Alienated Poor would normally never get a chance to realize

an average utility of 30. By their choice of a social arrangement, persons in the original positions would virtually fix their
social position for life. Consequently, even though both social
arrangements provide the same average utility, it would only
be rational for persons in the original position to be indifferent
between the two arrangements, if over the long run each person in the original position could in fact realize that average
utility to the same extent under both arrangements, and that
would require repeating the gamble a considerable number of
times, with an equal chance of turning up among the
Privileged Rich or among the Alienated Poor. But persons in
the original position do not have the opportunity of repeating
the gamble; they only have a choice of either realizing a utility
of 50 or a utility of 10 (Social Arrangement A') or realizing a
utility of 40 or a utility of 20 (Social Arrangement B'). Since
there is no possibility of realizing an average utility of 30,
Social Arrangement B', by guaranteeing each person in the
original position a significantly higher minimum, would
clearly be preferable.

It is important to realize that these preferences do not
accord with a principle of average utility which would
maximize average utility in society. A principle of average
utility would be indifferent between Social Arrangement A'
and Social Arrangement B', and the principle would select
Social Arrangement A over Social Arrangement B. But the
risk aversion of persons in the original position to entering a
one-time gamble that determines their life prospects would
lead them to have opposing preferences.

Needless to say, one could modify the restrictions imposed on the original position so as to bring the preferences of
persons in the original position in line with a principle of
average utility. One way to bring this about is to reconstitute
persons in the original position so that they would no longer be
facing a gamble that made it virtually impossible for them to
realize the average utility of their society. Thus one could

conceive of persons in the original position as living *seriatim* the lives or, better, integral parts of the lives of many randomly selected individuals in their society. In this way, each person in the original position, through his or her varied existence, would be able to realize, at least approximately, the average utility of their society. Consequently, they would no longer have any reason to be adverse to the one-time gamble facing them in the original position.

Yet this proposal for modifying the restrictions imposed on the original position simply exposes the inadequate conception of the nature of persons that underlies the principle of average utility. For in order to choose this principle, persons in the original position would have to think of themselves as living, *seriatim*, integral parts of the lives of many randomly selected individuals. To adopt the principle of average utility, therefore, would require that, at least for moral purposes, we begin to think of ourselves in a radically different way. In this connection, Rawls has argued that the principle of total utility, which would maximize total utility in society, also implies an inadequate conception of persons because that principle would be chosen by a sympathetic spectator who regards everyone's desires and satisfactions as if they were the desires and satisfactions of one person.[7] It could be argued, therefore, that both utilitarian principles fail to pay sufficient attention to the distinction between persons—the principle of total utility, by requiring that we think of ourselves as parts of one "total person"; the principle of average utility, by requiring that we think of ourselves as parts of what could be called "average persons."

In rejecting the maximin strategy and the principle of average utility, persons in the original position would implicitly be favoring an alternative conception of social cooperation. The maximin strategy, by ignoring the relevance of tradeoffs between parties at different levels of welfare, requires a minimum that would be regarded as too high by persons in the original position, while the principle of average utility, by focusing its concern on "average persons," could require a minimum that would be regarded as too low. Since persons in the original position would want to avoid the excesses of both views, they would choose to specify the minimum so as to compromise the requirements of both principles.

One way this could be done is by specifying the minimum in terms of the share of primary social goods that is necessary for satisfying a person's basic needs. If a person needs something, it must be the case that, with respect to some suitable standard, he would be deficient if he were not appropriately related to what he needs. Thus a person's basic needs are those needs which must be satisfied in order not to seriously endanger the person's health or sanity. The needs a person has for food, shelter, medical care, protection, companionship, and self-development are, at least in part, needs of this sort. Naturally, societies vary in their ability to satisfy a person's basic needs, but the needs themselves are not similarly subject to variation, unless there is a corresponding variation in what constitutes health and sanity in different societies.

Obviously, people have other needs that, in the above sense, are nonbasic. Some of these needs are functional or instrumental needs. For example, a barber needs a comb, scissors, and maybe a barber chair in order to cut hair; a carpenter needs lumber, a hammer, and maybe an electric saw in order to ply his trade; and a husband may need meat, potatoes, and certain other ingredients in order to prepare his wife's favorite stew. As in the last example, a person can have functional or instrumental needs for the same sort of goods he requires in order to satisfy his basic needs. Also, there can be serious disagreement as to what a person's functional or instrumental needs are. For example, de Jouvenel thought a professor's functional needs extend beyond his office and classroom and include the need to be able to entertain his colleagues and students in a comfortable manner,[8] whereas others would want to restrict a professor's functional needs to his office and classroom. It is not apparent how to resolve such disputes. Yet even if it were possible to reach agreement on what people's functional and instrumental needs are, it is clear that not all functional and instrumental needs ought to be satisfied. For example, a would-be safecracker may need dynamite and a fuse to blow up a safe, and a would-be murderer may need arsenic to poison his intended victim, but satisfying such functional or instrumental needs would not be morally justified. For these reasons, only when the criterion of need is restricted to basic needs does it appear to be an acceptable standard for determining the minimum amount of primary social goods a person should receive.

Actually, specifying a minimum of this sort seems to be the goal of the Poverty Index, used in the United States since 1964.[9] This index is based on the U.S. Department of Agriculture's Economy Food Plan (for an adequate diet) and on evidence that low-income families spend about one-third of their income on food, and is adjusted yearly to take changing prices into account. Thus, while a minimum that is defined in terms of a person's basic needs would generally (depending on what incentives are required to motivate people to contribute to society) be lower than the minimum required by the maximin strategy, it would not be unreasonably low when one considers that more than 24 million people in the United States fall below the poverty level.[10]

It is possible, of course, to specify a minimum in terms of a standard of living that is conventional and varies over time and among societies. Following this approach, Benn and Peters have suggested that an acceptable minimum could be specified in terms of the income received by the most numerous group in a society.[11] Specified in this manner, an acceptable minimum could be reached in some societies only by satisfying a considerable number of nonbasic needs. For example, in the United States today the greatest number of family units falls within the $15,000-$24,999 income bracket (in 1977 dollars).[12] Consequently, to specify a minimum in terms of this income group would provide for the satisfaction of many nonbasic needs. Moreover, suppose that the most numerous group of family units in a society that had the wealth of the United States fell within a $500-$999 income bracket (in 1977 dollars). Certainly it would not thereby follow that a guarantee of $1,000 per family unit would constitute an acceptable minimum for such a society. Or suppose that the income of the most numerous group of family units in such a society fell within the $95,000-$100,000 income bracket (in 1977 dollars). Certainly a minimum of $100,000 per family unit would not thereby be required. This suggests that an acceptable minimum is neither a direct function of the number of family units that share a particular income nor a direct function of the wealth of a particular society.

Nevertheless, it still seems that an acceptable minimum should vary over time and among societies, at least to some degree. For example, it could be argued that a television set is almost a necessity in the typical North American household today, which was not true thirty years ago, nor is it true today in most other countries of the world. Happily, a basic needs approach to defining an acceptable minimum can appropriately account for such variation. There is variation in the basic needs approach to defining an acceptable minimum, but the variation does not enter into the definition of the basic needs themselves, which are, for the most part, understood to be invariant over time and among societies. Instead, variation enters into the cost of satisfying those same needs at different times and in different societies,[13] for in the same society at different times, and in different societies at the same time, the normal costs of satisfying a person's basic needs can and do vary considerably. This is because the most readily available means for satisfying a person's basic needs in affluent societies are usually processed so as to satisfy certain nonbasic needs at the same time that they satisfy a person's basic needs. This processing is performed to make the means more attractive to persons in high income brackets, who can easily afford the extra cost. As a result, the most readily available means for satisfying a person's basic needs are much more costly in more affluent societies than in less affluent societies. This occurs most obviously with respect to the most readily available means for satisfying a person's basic needs for food, shelter, and transportation, but it also occurs with respect to the most readily available means for satisfying a person's basic needs for companionship, self-esteem, and self-development, for a person cannot normally satisfy even these latter needs in more affluent societies without participating in some relatively costly educational and social development practices. Thus there can be considerable variation in the normal costs of satisfying a person's basic needs as a society becomes more affluent over time, and at any time in societies at different levels of affluence. Consequently, a basic needs approach to defining an acceptable minimum would guarantee a person the primary social goods that are necessary to meet the normal costs of satisfying his basic needs in the society in which he lives.

Nor would it be reasonable for persons in the original position to require the members of an affluent society to do more for those in the lower income brackets of their society than provide a basic needs minimum. The reason for this, as we shall see later in this chapter and more particularly in Chapter 6, is that making provision for the basic needs of future generations and distant peoples would take precedence over further assistance to those whose basic needs have already been met. Given what we know about the world's resources, after provision is made for the basic needs of future generations and distant peoples, little will be left for further assistance to those whose basic needs have already been met.

In summary, then, persons in the original position would have the following reasons for favoring a minimum that is defined in terms of a person's basic needs:

1) A basic needs minimum is generally lower than the minimum required by the maximin strategy yet high enough to require significant redistribution in most affluent societies.
2) A basic needs minimum allows for variation in the cost of satisfying a person's basic needs over time and among societies, without making the minimum simply a function of the number of people who share a particular income or the wealth of a particular society.
3) Going beyond a basic needs minimum in more affluent societies is not an acceptable alternative, once the basic needs of future generations and distant peoples are taken into account.

On the basis of these reasons, persons in the original position would find it rational to accept the following principle of distributive justice:

Principle of Need: Each person is guaranteed the primary social goods that are necessary to meet the normal costs of satisfying his basic needs in the society in which he lives.

Under favorable conditions, where there are sufficient social and economic resources and the incentive to contribute to society would not be adversely affected, the Principle of Need would guarantee a minimum to everyone in society, without requiring even a minimal contribution to society from those who are capable of contributing—unless it could be shown that realizing a person's conception of the good life does not conflict with making a minimal contribution to society.

The choice of an acceptable minimum by persons in the original position leads immediately to the question of how primary social goods are to be distributed over and above the minimum. With an acceptable minimum guaranteed, persons in the original position would be interested in choosing principles of distribution that provide them with more, rather than fewer, primary social goods. To achieve that result, they would want to provide the members of their society with the incentive necessary to maximize their contribution to society, and the most obvious way of providing that incentive is by distributing additional primary social goods on the basis of a person's contribution to society. The problem, of course, is how to determine a person's contribution to society. Obviously, in order to provide each person in society with an acceptable minimum of primary social goods, it may be necessary to distribute primary social goods on the basis of a person's contribution to the production of primary economic goods (i.e., income and wealth). Yet once an acceptable minimum has been provided, it is less clear that the distribution of additional primary social goods should continue to be based primarily on a person's contribution to economic production. Rather, with an acceptable minimum secured, persons in the original position who want the members of their society to have the incentive necessary to maximize their various contributions to society would do far better to let additional primary social goods be distributed on the basis of private appropriation and voluntary agreement and exchange.[14] This process of private appropriation and voluntary agreement and exchange would probably continue to result in increased production of primary economic goods, but it could just as well encourage artistic, cultural, and scientific contributions to society that have little or no economic value. Moreover, the provision of primary social goods that are necessary to meet the basic needs of all the members of a society, as well as the provision of primary social goods to meet the basic needs of future generations and distant peoples, would provide sufficient background constraints against the accumulation of wealth and power in the hands of a few through this process of private appropriation and voluntary agreement and exchange. For these reasons, assuming that the Principle of Need has been satisfied, persons in the original position would want the following principle to govern the distribution of primary social goods:

> *Principle of Appropriation and Exchange:* Additional primary social goods are to be distributed on the basis of private appropriation and voluntary agreement and exchange.

It has been noted before that when social and economic resources are insufficient to provide everyone with a guaranteed minimum or when the incentive to contribute to society would be adversely affected, so that persons would not maximize their contribution to society, then those who are capable of contributing to society would be required to make a minimal contribution in order to receive the share of primary social goods that are necessary for satisfying their basic needs. Since persons normally cannot do without that share of primary social goods, the ordinary person has no choice but to contribute. Yet even when there are sufficient social and economic resources and incentive would not be adversely affected if each person were provided with an acceptable minimum, irrespective of whether he made any contribution to society, some contribution may still be required if it could be shown that those capable individuals who are not contributing to society are also not realizing a conception of the good life that would conflict with making a minimal contribution to society. If we assume, however, that under these favorable conditions it would not be necessary to require a minimal contribution from those who are capable of contributing, then persons in the original position would favor the following principle:

> *Principle of Minimal Contribution:* A minimal contribution to society is required of those who are capable of contributing when social and economic resources are insufficient to provide the guaranteed minimum to everyone in society without requiring that contribution or when the incentive to contribute to society would oth-

erwise be adversely affected, so that persons would not maximize their contribution to society.

An important problem that is yet to be considered is determining an acceptable rate of "saving" from the point of view of the original position. Societies save by increasing their social and economic resources, which include factories, machines, and technical and humanistic knowledge, while preserving their natural resources. For there to be such saving, it is necessary that the increase in social and economic resources be coupled with an economical use of natural resources. Even an enormous increase in social and economic resources cannot compensate for a totally depleted supply of natural resources. The *rate* of saving between generations in a society, then, is determined by comparing the saving each generation passes along to the next generation, along with the social, economic and natural resources it received from the preceding generations, and an acceptable rate of saving between generations would certainly depend on the society's level of social and economic development. For when societies are largely primitive and agrarian, the acceptable rate is lower than it is when societies become highly cultured and industrialized. It also seems reasonable to assume that when social and economic resources have been sufficiently accumulated, so as to permit all members of a society to benefit fully from their just institutions, then no further saving would be required. At such a time, the acceptable rate of saving would be zero.

We might, therefore, specify the acceptable rate of saving the following way:

> *Principle of Saving:* The rate of saving for each generation should represent its fair contribution toward realizing and maintaining a society in which all the members can fully enjoy the benefit of its just institutions.

Rawls also seems to be arguing in favor of a similar principle of saving.[15] Nevertheless, there is an important difference between our theories. Rawls thinks that such a principle would be chosen in the original position, given his characterization of that position, while I maintain that it would be chosen only if Rawls' characterization of the original position is modified.

Given Rawls' description of the original position, although persons so situated do not know to which generation they belong, they *do* know that they are contemporaries. Consequently, it would be reasonable for them to favor their own generation by refusing to accept the Principle of Saving and the sacrifices it entails. Previous generations have either saved or they have not, and by agreeing in the present to the Principle of Saving, persons in the original position can in no way affect how they were treated by previous generations.[16] Persons in the original position may have self-interested and self-glorifying reasons for providing the next generation with a certain supply of capital and natural resources, but such reasons would clearly not be sufficient to motivate them to choose the Principle of Saving. Rawls is certainly aware of this problem and, in order to handle it, postulates that persons in the original position are at least interested in the welfare of the next generation. Yet, since Rawls does not specify how interested persons in the original position are in the welfare of the next generation, it is unclear whether they would come to any unanimous agreement on an acceptable rate of saving. In any case, they would not have sufficient reason to make the sacrifices required by the Principle of Saving because they are only (to an unspecified degree) benevolently interested in the next generation. Later generations are beyond the concern of persons in the original position, except insofar as the welfare of subsequent generations would contribute to the welfare of the immediate descendants of those in the original position. This would not provide sufficient grounds to motivate the accumulation of social and economic resources and the preservation of natural resources required by the Principle of Saving. The fact that they do not know to which generation they belong is of no help. As was said before, the decisions of persons in the original position, who are contemporaries, can have no effect upon how they were treated by earlier generations. Thus, given Rawls' characterization of the original position, persons so situated would only adopt a plan for using resources that benefited themselves and the next generation but paid little or no account to the interest of succeeding generations. They would not choose the Principle of Saving.

There is, however, a fairly simple way of making it in the interest of persons in the original position to choose the Principle of Saving. In fact, this can be done without assuming that persons in the original position have any benevolent interests at all, not even benevolent interests in the welfare of their immediate descendants. All that is required to make it in the interest of persons in the original position to choose the Principle of Saving is an extension of the veil of ignorance, so that persons in the original position do not know whether they are contemporaries or whether they belong to some unspecified future generation. If the veil of ignorance is drawn in this fashion, it would be in the self-interest of persons in the original position to choose the Principle of Saving. They may well turn out to be in one of the future generations, and hence it is in their interest to secure a reasonable rate of saving and guard against a reckless use of natural resources.[17]

Rawls briefly discusses the possibility of characterizing the original position as including all those who *will* live at some time or even *could* live at some time; he claims that both of these alternatives are intuitively implausible. Certainly, it is not easy to comprehend what principles would be acceptable to people who know that they might be dead or might only possibly be alive at some time; but to conceive of persons in the original position as either contemporaries or as belonging to an unspecified future generation does not seem to involve comparable difficulties. Also, this modification of the original position accords with the rationale for introducing the veil of ignorance in the first place, which was to remove from consideration facts of special interest in making decisions in conflict-of-interest situations. Moreover, this modification has no effect on the choice of the other principles of distributive justice. The same considerations which would motivate acceptance of those principles continue to apply. Only the choice of an acceptable rate of saving is affected by modifying the original position in this way.

This completes my account of the principles of distributive justice that would be chosen by persons in the (now modified) original position. They are, to recapitulate, the following:

Principle of Need: Each person is guaranteed the primary social goods that are necessary to meet the normal costs of satisfying his basic needs in the society in which he lives. (The Principle of Need applies under the assumption that there are sufficient social and economic resources in the society to maintain the guaranteed minimum, but not necessarily without requiring a minimal contribution to society.)

Principle of Appropriation and Exchange: Additional primary social goods are to be distributed on the basis of private appropriation and voluntary agreement and exchange.

Principle of Minimal Contribution: A minimal contribution to society is required of those who are capable of contributing, when social and economic resources are insufficient to provide the guaranteed minimum to everyone in society without requiring that contribution or when the incentive to contribute to society would otherwise be adversely affected, so that persons would not maximize their contribution to society.

Principle of Saving: The rate of saving for each generation should represent its fair contribution toward realizing and maintaining a society in which the members can fully enjoy the benefit of its just institutions.

The choice of these principles by persons in the original position reflects their desire to arrange the distribution of primary social goods so that, provided they are guaranteed an acceptable minimum whatever their position in society, their share of primary social goods is as large as it can possibly be for that position—assuming, that is, that they are making their maximal contribution to society. This is the strategy that persons in the original position would employ in choosing the above principles. The acceptable minimum is determined by the Principle of Need and the Principle of Saving and is secured by the Principle of Minimal Contribution, while the Principle of Appropriation and Exchange distributes additional primary social goods so as to make the share of primary social goods of each contributing member of society as large as possible.

These principles have been derived from a commonly accepted ideal of justice as fairness, which only requires that we discount facts of special interest in reaching decisions in conflict-of-interest situations. Although Rawls' hypothetical choice situation or original position was used to draw out the implications of this moral ideal, the derived principles are quite distinct from the principles Rawls defends. What has been shown is that commitment to this commonly accepted ideal of justice as fairness requires neither utilitarian nor maximin principles of distributive justice but rather principles that place the acceptable minimum between those extremes. In the next chapter, this commonly accepted ideal will be used to determine principles of retributive justice.

3. Retributive Justice

IN RECENT YEARS, attempts to defend retributive theories of punishment against utilitarianism have taken a variety of forms. Some have defended retributivism as a logical doctrine; others have argued that retributivism is a necessary and sufficient moral requirement for a system of punishment; still others have maintained that retributivism is only a necessary moral requirement for a system of punishment. The standard utilitarian response to such attempts has been to claim that once the relevant retributive principles have been purged of any morally unacceptable features (such as *lex talionis* vengefulness), those principles can always be justified in terms of the maximization of utility. In this chapter I wish to show that this standard utilitarian response, while quite successful in countering most versions of retributivism, cannot meet the challenge of the ideal of justice as fairness, captured by John Rawls' decision procedure.

Versions of Retributivism

The version of retributivism that is most compatible with utilitarianism is retributivism understood as a logical doctrine. This form of retributivism is simply a thesis about the definition of punishment. It maintains that retributivism is essentially the view that punishment, by definition, can only be inflicted on the guilty. So understood, retributivism "is not a

moral but a logical doctrine,'' and ''it does not provide a moral
justification of the infliction of punishment but an elucidation
of the use of the word.'' Obviously, this version of retributivism, being simply a thesis about the meaning of the word
''punishment,'' presents no problem for the utilitarian. Some
actions that are justified on utilitarian grounds will satisfy this
definition of punishment and others will not, but the proposed
definition does not in any way determine which actions are
morally justified. Moreover, objections to the adequacy of this
definition (e.g., that punishment of the innocent is logically
impossible) can be taken up entirely within a utilitarian
framework. No matter how the definitional question is settled,
the acceptability of utilitarianism is left unchallenged.

Retributivism as a logical doctrine has little in common
with the traditional retributive view of Kant and Hegel. In the
traditional view, retributivism is a moral and not simply a
logical doctrine. Its basic tenet is that punishing a person is
morally justified if and only if the person committed an offense
for which he or she deserves punishment. This traditional view
professes to provide a justification of punishment that is incompatible with utilitarianism. That incompatibility is clearly
brought out by Kant in the following passage from *The
Metaphysics of Morals:*

> Even if a civil society resolved to dissolve itself with the
> consent of all its members—as might be supposed in the
> case of a people inhabiting an island resolving to separate
> and scatter themselves throughout the whole world—the
> last murderer lying in prison ought to be executed before
> the resolution was carried out. This ought to be done in
> order that everyone may realize the desert of his deeds,
> and that blood-guiltiness may not remain upon the
> people; for otherwise they will all be regarded as par-
> ticipators in the murder as a public violation of justice.[1]

Variations of this traditional view have recently been
defended against utilitarianism. J. D. Mabbot, noting that the

concept of punishment is primarily at home in legal contexts, has attempted to defend a legalistic version of the traditional retributive thesis. He maintains that the only justification for punishing any man is that he has broken the law.[2] C. W. K. Mundle has tried to improve upon Mabbot's formulation, claiming that punishing a person is morally justified if and only if the person in breaking the law committed a moral offense.[3] And certainly an attractive variation of the traditional thesis, put forward by H. J. McCloskey, maintains that for punishing a person to be morally justified it is *generally* (but not always) necessary and sufficient that the person committed an offense for which he deserves punishment.[4] McCloskey's modification of the traditional thesis allows for the possibility that considerations of social consequences may sometimes override a retributive justification of punishment.

Nevertheless, the traditional retributive view has not fared well in its debate with utilitarianism. Ted Honderich, in his survey of justification for punishment, observes:

> There no longer are defenders of the traditional retributive theory. . . . At any rate, there are no defenders writing in the usual places.[5]

The basic problem has been that the traditional view, insofar as it differs from utilitarianism with respect to the social institutions it justifies, often appears simply to be attempting to justify a form of revenge. For example, many have regarded Kant's justification for executing every murderer before dissolving a society as nothing more than a defense of institutionalized revenge. Quite possibly, McCloskey has formulated his own version of the retributive thesis to take account of such problem cases, since (presumably) the absence of any good social consequences from the execution of murderers at the dissolution of a society would be sufficient, in McCloskey's view, to override a retributive justification for such punishment. Yet if the traditional retributive view is modified in this manner to take into account consideration of social consequences, it becomes difficult to see how the view, so modified, provides any practical recommendations different from utilitarianism or presents a superior moral justification for punishment. Accordingly, Mundle has recently suggested that all he wishes to retain from his retributive position might well be justified within a utilitarian framework; and others have argued that whenever utilitarianism conflicts with traditional retributivism, it is the utilitarian view that is morally justified.

To avoid the problems of traditional retributivism, a number of contemporary philosophers have favored a form of retributivism that imposes only a generally necessary moral requirement on the justification of punishment. H. L. A. Hart, one of the most prominent proponents of this view, holds that, in general, punishment is morally justified only if it is inflicted on a person who has committed an offense with *mens rea* (i.e., knowledge of circumstances, foresight of consequences, and voluntariness).[6] Hart contends that this requirement cannot be supported simply on utilitarian grounds.

According to Hart, considerations of deterrence could lead a utilitarian to punish people who acted without mens rea. For example, it may be that people who know that they will be held strictly liable for committing certain offenses will tend to take additional precautions to avoid those offenses, thus resulting in greater conformity to the law. In fact, military discipline seems to have this sort of effect on soldiers. For this reason, Hart claims that in order to justify restricting punishment to persons who have committed offenses with mens rea, a nonutilitarian justification is required and, in his view, that justification can be provided by a criterion of fairness. To give people a fair opportunity of adjusting their behavior to the law, Hart argues, it is generally necessary to restrict punishment to those who have committed offenses with mens rea. It is claimed that this restriction would not be acceptable to a utilitarian.

At first glance, Hart's case against utilitarianism looks quite strong. The restriction of punishment to persons who have committed offenses with mens rea is a feature of our system of punishment that we generally find morally justified. In most cases we would not think it right to sacrifice this feature, even if it could be shown that greater deterrence would result. Consequently, if utilitarianism required such a sacrifice, we would certainly have reason to think it an inadequate moral theory. In fact, however, it can be shown that utilitarianism roughly conforms with many of our moral intuitions concerning requirements for a system of punishment. They appeared drastically different in Hart's discussion only because Hart failed to take account of certain social consequences in determining what system of punishment a utilitarian would regard as justified. For in addition to considering the consequences of deterrence, a utilitarian would also consider the satisfactions people would derive from having certain restrictions built into their system of punishment, such as the satisfaction of knowing that they will not generally be punished if, sheerly by accident, they commit a crime. When all the relevant consequences are taken into account, therefore, it is not clear that a utilitarian would have to reject Hart's form of retributivism.

In general, then, the utilitarian response to forms of retributivism appears to be quite successful. It has not seemed implausible to argue that when traditional retributivism is purged of its morally unacceptable vengefulness (as occurs, for example, in Hart's form of retributivism), then the view can be justified in terms of the maximization of utility. Nevertheless, I propose to show that there is a morally adequate form of retributivism that can be justified in terms of fairness but not in terms of utility. This, of course, is what Hart wanted to establish. In what follows, I hope to show that Rawls' decision procedure can be used to support Hart's view.

The Use of Rawls' Decision Procedure

To understand how Rawls' decision procedure can be applied, imagine we were trying to determine fair principles for governing the relationships between judges, police officers, prison officials, criminals, victims of crime, and the general public—that is, every member of society insofar as he or she has an interest in our legal enforcement system. We might begin (assuming it were practically possible) by having a general meeting of representatives of all the relevant interests. Such a meeting, if each representative were given a chance to argue in favor of his or her particular interests, might result in greater appreciation of all the relevant viewpoints. However, it would be unrealistic to think that a meeting of this sort would necessarily result in the selection of fair principles for governing the relationships among all the represented parties. As at the comparable meeting of representatives to determine principles of distributive justice, the chance of that occurring would be very slight, unless there were some way to carry on deliberations at the meeting so that each relevant interest received its "proper weight" from a moral point of view. For if fair decisions are to be achieved, the method of reaching decisions must go beyond the number of individuals supporting each interest and take into account the relative importance of majority and minority interests. It is this morally acceptable result that Rawls' decision procedure is designed to produce.

Suppose, then, we were to employ Rawls' decision procedure at the meeting where all those who have an interest in our legal enforcement system are represented. Each person at the meeting would be attempting to reach a decision as to the principles he favors for governing the legal enforcement system while imagining himself to be ignorant of his own special interests. Judges, for example, would imagine themselves to be ignorant of the fact that they are judges and would attempt to decide what principles they would find acceptable, assuming it were possible that they might turn out to occupy any of the relevant positions having an interest in the legal enforcement system. The other representatives at the meeting would employ the same method of discounting their own special interests. Given the availability of information for assessing each of the represented interests and the ability of each of the parties to rationally assess that information, this method of decision making would culminate in a unanimous decision. This is because each representative would be deliberating in a rationally correct manner with respect to the same information and would be using a decision procedure leading to a uniform evaluation of the alternatives, consequently, all would favor the same principles for governing their legal enforcement system.

While this decision procedure is designed to secure the choice of principles that are fair, it can be shown that the principles that would be chosen by this method would not have the effect of maximizing utility in society. Representatives at the meeting of all those who have an interest in the legal enforcement system would certainly consider the possibility of selecting principles that maximize utility. However, a necessary requirement for selecting them would be that the representatives did not experience any risk aversion when they imagined themselves as possibly turning up in any of the represented positions in a system which maximized utility— possibly even turning up as a criminal or a victim of crime. Any risk aversion whatsoever would favor the choice of principles that sacrificed average or total utility to improve the conditions of the least desirable positions or that lessened the chance of a person's occupying those positions. Yet for the representatives *not* to experience any risk aversion, they would have to be convinced that maximizing utility would guarantee a sufficiently high minimum of utility to those in the least desirable positions in society. What needs to be determined, therefore, is whether the guarantee of a sufficiently high minimum of utility for those in the least desirable positions would obtain under a legal enforcement system that maximized utility.

Let us begin by imagining a society, analogous to the society considered in Chapter 2, in which there are two major social groups: the Legal Gainers, that is, those who are secure and prosperous in the society, and the Legal Losers, that is, those who are punished or victimized in the society. We need not assume that everyone in the society belongs to one or the other of these two groups (some persons in the society may be neither safe and prosperous nor punished or victimized), but let us assume that the combined utility of the members of these two groups virtually determines the utility of the whole society. Suppose further that, using Rawls' decision procedure, persons would assign the following utility values to representative members of these two groups under alternative social arrangements.

	Social Arrangement A	Social Arrangement B
Legal Gainers	55	40
Legal Losers	10	20

	Social Arrangement A'	Social Arrangement B'
Legal Gainers	50	40
Legal Losers	10	20

Now if persons, using Rawls' decision procedure, were to favor maximizing utility in this society, they would select Social Arrangement A over Social Arrangement B and they would be indifferent between Social Arrangement A' and Social Arrangement B'. However, it was argued in Chapter 2 that persons using Rawls' decision procedure would have reason to favor Social Arrangement B over Social Arrangement A and Social Arrangement B' over Social Arrangement A'. The justification was that since persons in such a society would not have a chance to realize the average utility of each social arrangement but would only be able to realize either the higher or the lower utility value, persons using Rawls' decision procedure would prefer the two social arrangements with the higher minimum utility values. Another way to put the same point is that persons using Rawls' decision procedure would be risk averse to the lower minimum utility values of Social Arrangement A and Social Arrangement A', even though, with respect to maximizing utility in such a society, these social arrangements are equally good or better than their alternatives. This was the basis for concluding that Rawls' decision procedure would rule out the selection of utilitarian principles.

But a utilitarian who was attracted to the ideal of justice as fairness would certainly want to resist this conclusion, for it would mean that, in consistency, he would have to give up either his commitment to the ideal of justice as fairness or his commitment to utilitarianism. Hoping to avoid this result, a utilitarian might admit that persons using Rawls' decision procedure would prefer Social Arrangement B over Social Arrangement A and Social Arrangement B' over Social Arrangement A', but then deny that this would serve to show the incompatibility of the ideal of justice as fairness with utilitarianism, on the grounds that these social arrangements do not constitute a realistic set of alternatives. Thus a utilitarian might claim that, to demonstrate the incompatibility of the ideal of justice as fairness with utilitarianism, it must be shown that a sufficiently high minimum of utility would not be the realistic outcome of a legal enforcement system that maximized utility.

For example, consider Social Arrangement A and Social Arrangement B. With respect to this set of alternatives, a utilitarian might claim that under realistic conditions there would be the possibility of a third alternative, Social Arrangement C, that would both provide at least as high a minimum of utility as Social Arrangement B and a greater total utility than Social Arrangement A. This third alternative, Social Arrangement C, would be said to result from transferring from the Legal Gainers to the Legal Losers sufficient primary social goods to secure a minimum of utility that is at least as high as that provided by Social Arrangement B. Such a transfer—assuming uniform declining marginal utility—would be said to provide greater utility to the Legal Losers than to the Legal Gainers, thus rendering Social Arrangement C preferable to Social Arrangement A on utilitarian grounds.

But is it reasonable to assume that a transfer of primary social goods producing just these results is realistically possible? There are a number of reasons for thinking that this is not the case.

First of all, under realistic conditions might not a significant fraction of the utility enjoyed by the Legal Gainers derive not directly from the larger shares of primary social goods they possess but rather from the fact that they have considerably more primary social goods than the Legal Losers? But if under realistic conditions this were the case, then raising the minimum in Social Arrangement A to match that in Social Arrangement B would tend to collapse Social Arrangement A into Social Arrangement B, producing a net loss of utility. Since this would mean that Social Arrangement A would remain the preferred utilitarian alternative, persons using Rawls' decision procedure would still have reason to select Social Arrangement B.

Secondly, even if under realistic conditions there is a Social Arrangement C that would provide at least as high a minimum of utility as Social Arrangement B and a greater total utility than Social Arrangement A, might not the only acceptable utilitarian method for transforming a society under Social Arrangement A into a society under Social Arrangement C necessitate a gradual transition, so as not to sharply decrease the utility experienced by Legal Gainers who have grown accustomed to their preferred status? But if this were the case, persons using Rawls' decision procedure would have reason to reject, not Social Arrangement C itself, but the acceptable utilitarian method of bringing about such an arrangement. For persons using Rawls' decision procedure would want a sufficiently high minimum of utility to be secured directly and immediately, regardless of whether a rapid transition would decrease total utility.[7]

Thirdly, how realistic is the assumption of uniform declining marginal utility of primary social goods? While it seems reasonable to grant that everyone experiences some sort of decline in the marginal utility of primary social goods, utilitarians, to approximate the ideal of justice as fairness, must go further and assume that the decline occurs uniformly for everyone, either immediately before or at least immediately after his basic needs are satisfied. (For example, it won't do if the decline occurs only after a yearly income between $35,000 and $50,000 is attained.) In defending this assumption, however, utilitarians don't usually claim *to know* that declining marginal utility occurs uniformly at an early stage in the acquisition of primary social goods.[8] Usually they claim that, given the uncertainties of determining the rates of declining marginal utility for particular individuals, it is best *to assume* that the decline occurs uniformly for everyone at an early stage in the acquisition of primary social goods. Of course, at this point one might wonder whether those who accept this assumption on such grounds are really basing their normative judgments on utility assessments after all. Yet even disregarding this point, it is still far from clear that we don't have good evidence in many cases of significant differences in declining marginal utility of primary social goods. Thus increased skill at assessing these differences might well open up the possibility of maximizing utility by distributing a scarce supply of primary social goods primarily to the members of one subgroup within a society (e.g., the Legal Gainers) instead of making sure that everyone in the society has a sufficiently high minimum of utility.

Lastly, and most importantly, even if it were reasonable to assume that uniform declining marginal utility occurs at an early stage in the acquisition of primary social goods, and even if a legal enforcement system that maximizes utility always provided a relatively high minimum of utility, and even if a utilitarian transition to such a legal enforcement system would always be direct and immediate, it still would not be the case that persons using Rawls' decision procedure would regard as sufficient the minimum that is guaranteed by maximizing utility. For given the importance of this choice to the life prospects of the persons choosing in imagined ignorance of their special interests, it would be reasonable for them to adopt a somewhat conservative stance and choose principles that sacrifice total utility (to some degree) for the sake of an even higher minimum of utility. This conservative stance would not lead to the choice of the highest possible minimum of utility, but the risks involved would lead to the sacrifice of some total utility for the sake of a higher minimum of utility.[9]

On the basis of the above considerations, therefore, persons using Rawls' decision procedure would have reason to doubt whether a relatively high minimum of utility would be the realistic outcome of a legal enforcement system that maximizes utility, and even if they were to disregard those doubts they would still have reason to secure a somewhat higher minimum than a legal enforcement system that maximizes utility could provide. On this account, persons using Rawls' decision procedure would experience at least some risk aversion to occupying the undesirable positions in a society that maximizes utility. Hence it would be rational for the representatives of all who have an interest in the legal enforcement system, when choosing in imagined ignorance of their special interests, to favor principles that reflect their degree of risk aversion over principles that maximize utility in society.

Of course, Rawls' decision procedure could be reconstructed so that it would lead to utilitarian principles for legal enforcement. But the only way that this could be done, other than by reconstituting persons using Rawls' decision procedure, is by stipulating that persons using the procedure have no aversion to risk when considering what positions they might occupy. Yet this requirement, unlike the ignorance condition, is not needed to ensure fairness; it is simply a means of ensuring the choice of utilitarian principles. To introduce the requirement is to beg the question as to the nature of the conflict between fairness and utility. While fairness can be interpreted as requiring an ignorance condition, an ignorance condition, unless qualified by a restriction ruling out risk aversion, will not lead to the choice of utilitarian principles.

Moreover, if we drop the assumption that persons using Rawls' decision procedure are choosing for realistic conditions, then the differences between the ideal of justice as fairness and utilitarianism become even more striking. For representatives using Rawls' decision procedure would still want the guarantee of a sufficiently high minimum of utility for each person in society, even if, for example, they assumed that declining marginal utility of primary social goods did not occur until persons acquired a yearly income of well over $100,000. Thus, while such an assumption would drastically alter the normative implications of utilitarianism, it would leave the requirements of justice as fairness relatively unaffected.

Principles of Retributive Justice

But what sort of principles would representatives to the meeting of all those who have an interest in the legal enforcement system choose, using Rawls' decision procedure? First of all, they would want their legal enforcement system to have certain safeguards against punishing behavior that was excusable for reasons of accident, mistake, provocation, duress, or insanity. This means they would favor Hart's principle that punishment is generally morally justified only if it is inflicted on a person who has committed an offense with the cognitive and volitional conditions of mens rea. In their imagined ignorance, accepting such a principle would be the best way of safeguarding their own interests, since they would have no way of assessing with confidence the probability of their being accused of a crime in which excusing conditions would be relevant. Unless a legal system with excusing conditions were adopted, there would be very little a representative could do to protect himself against such a possibility. While under normal conditions a person can avoid killing someone deliberately, there is very little a person can do to avoid killing someone accidentally or harming him while under hypnosis or in an epileptic fit. Furthermore, the representatives would not be impressed by the gains in deterrence attainable by eliminating or restricting the use of excusing conditions, since in their imagined ignorance they would have no grounds for thinking that they themselves might not commit a serious offense in circumstances where excusing conditions would be relevant. In fact, the representatives' risk aversion to finding themselves in such an unfortunate position would lead them (for the reasons previously given) to favor safeguards stronger than anything that could be defended simply in terms of the maximization of utility.

On the same account, the representatives would find it rational to choose a legal system that contained procedural safeguards against punishing the innocent, such as the requirement of conduct, the presumption of innocence, and the evidential restrictions of due process.[10] Again, these legal safeguards would be specified in such a way that they would provide each individual with firmer guarantees against being wrongfully punished than could be justified in terms of the maximization of utility.

But clearly, the choice situation facing the representatives of all those who have an interest in the legal enforcement system is more complicated than the one that would be facing representatives at a comparable meeting of those seeking to determine principles of distributive justice. At each of these meetings, it would be important to determine the least advantaged position, since the representatives—because of their risk aversion to their choice situation—would want to secure an acceptable minimum well-being for persons occupying that position. At the meeting of those seeking to determine principles of distributive justice, however, there would not be competing candidates for the least advantaged position (even though there would be difficulties determining the well-being of persons in that position). In contrast, at the meeting of all who have an interest in the legal enforcement system, there would be at least two plausible candidates for the least advantaged position, that of the criminal and that of the victim of crime; and obviously, persons occupying those positions would have opposing interests. Since the representatives would be making their choice in imagined ignorance of their own special interests, it would not be rational for them completely to disregard the interests of either group. Nevertheless, the representatives would have grounds for favoring the interests of the victim of crime over those of the criminal as long as the legal system has adequate safeguards against punishing the innocent and a defensible system of excusing conditions, and as long as the laws of the society are reasonably just, as determined by the representatives to the meeting of those seeking principles of distributive justice. For under those conditions, the criminal's undesirable position would have resulted from his decision to violate the rights of others. Unlike the victim, the criminal would have been able to avoid his fate if he had chosen to abide by the reasonably just laws of the society.

Recognizing this fact, the representatives, deciding on principles of retributive justice, would wish to adopt measures to protect the interests of the victim, even when this involved sacrificing those of the criminal. Although the representatives would be choosing in imagined ignorance of their own position in society, they still would favor the interests of the victim of crime over those of the criminal. That is why the principles they would choose would differ from utilitarian principles. From a utilitarian point of view, the suffering of the victim would have to be weighed equally with the suffering of the criminal in determining the legal system that maximized utility, fulfilling Bentham's principle, "Each person counts for one, nobody for more than one." From the point of view of representatives deciding on principles of retributive justice, however, there would be grounds for rejecting this utilitarian solution.

But knowing that the interests of the criminal are not to be weighed equally with those of the victim is not sufficient to fix the amount of punishment that the representatives would choose to inflict on the criminal. Needless to say, in making this determination the representatives would certainly want to restrict the extent to which the criminal's interests could be sacrificed in order to provide an effective legal enforcement system. One possible limit has recently been proposed by Claudia Card.[11] It requires that the penalty not exceed the worst that anyone could reasonably be expected to suffer from the similar conduct of another if such conduct were to become general in the community—general in that it is engaged in by all those who, in the present circumstances, are taken unfair advantage of by the criminal. The idea behind this proposal is that some crimes (such as tax evasion) may fail to cause any harm (or at least any significant harm) only because they take place in a context of general obedience to the laws they violate. Obviously, this is not something for which the criminal can take credit; hence this view maintains that the full

measure of punishment should not be determined by the harm
a crime causes in such favorable circumstances but rather by
the worst harm that similar conduct could reasonably be expected to cause in a context of general disobedience. For
crimes such as murder, of course, there would be no difference, but for crimes such as breach of contract there would
be a significant difference.

While the rationale for this standard is not without its
appeal, there are two basic difficulties with using the standard
to determine the maximum amount of punishment that may be
legitimately inflicted on the criminal. The first stems from the
fact that it would be virtually impossible for any cooperative
practice, faced with general disobedience or noncompliance of
all who are taken unfair advantage of by the criminal, to per-
sist. Under such conditions, the practice would simply cease,
and the harm that an act of noncompliance would contribute to
would be the disastrous loss of the practice itself, with all its
benefits. Consequently, if a criminal's hypothetical contribution to such disastrous losses were used to determine the
maximum allowable penalty, it is difficult to see how any
penalty would be excluded, except possibly the death sen-
tence. In effect, then, the proposed standard would not prove
useful for scaling the amount of punishment that may be inflicted on criminals for the various crimes they might commit.

The second difficulty with the proposed standard is that
it fails to distinguish between cases where the representatives
might choose to hold a person liable for punishment that is
equal to the worst possible consequences of his action and
cases where something else would be required. For instance,
the representatives might favor holding a person who has been
convicted of attempted murder liable for punishment that is
equal to the harm his action would have caused if he had
succeeded in killing his intended victim. Yet, at the same time,
the representatives would be against holding a person who
failed to pay his taxes, under conditions of general com-

pliance, liable to punishment equal to the worst possible consequences of his action under conditions of general noncompliance.

The reason the representatives would treat these cases differently is that they would find it rational to hold a person liable for punishment equal to the worst possible consequences of his action only *if,* had those consequences been actual, they also found it rational to hold the person liable for that same amount of punishment. This requirement, which the representatives would consider to be in everyone's interest, permits the use of Card's standard in cases of attempted murder, but not in cases of tax evasion. For under circumstances where others generally do not pay their taxes, little good would come from a particular person's paying his. Consequently, for those circumstances, the representatives would not choose to hold a person liable for punishment equal to the worst consequences of his act of noncompliance, even if his act contributed to the collapse of most governmental functions. This is not to say that a person would not be regarded as having an obligation to do his part to restore governmental functions (maybe by meeting with people and getting them to agree to support certain local services). Yet since, for conditions of general noncompliance, the representatives would not choose to hold a person liable for punishment equal to the worst consequences of his failing to pay his taxes, it follows, given their acceptance of the above requirement, that they would not choose to hold the person liable to that amount of punishment for conditions where the actual consequences of his failing to pay his taxes were considerably less harmful. The difficulty with Card's standard, therefore, is that by being too general it fails to distinguish between cases such as tax evasion, where the offense is primarily against fairness and where the representatives would not choose to hold a person liable for punishment equal in severity to the worst possible consequences of his action, and other cases such as those of attempted murder or attempted robbery, where the offense is closely connected with consequences and the representative might be inclined to match the punishment with the worst possible consequences of the action. Consequently, even if the first difficulty could be overcome, and the proposed standard could be used to scale the amount of punishment that may be inflicted on criminals for the various crimes they might commit, this second difficulty would remain, providing representatives choosing principles of retributive justice with sufficient grounds for rejecting the standard.

To put the matter more positively, the strategy the representatives would adopt in selecting principles of retributive justice would be to place certain limits on the pursuit of utilitarian goals. For example, when properly qualified, they would favor the following principle for determining the amount of punishment to be inflicted on a criminal:

> *Principle of Deterrence:* Punishment is to be generally restricted to the least amount of harm sufficient 1) to maintain general deterrence among those who would be tempted to commit similar crimes and 2) to prevent recidivism among criminals.

Sometimes, punishments that are sufficient to maintain general deterrence among those who would be tempted to commit similar crimes (e.g., punishments severe enough to deter drunken driving) would also be sufficient to prevent recidivism; for other crimes (e.g. murder and assault), this would not obtain. Hence both conditions must be considered in determining the amount of punishment.

Utilitarians who make appropriate assumptions might also be inclined to accept this principle for limiting punishment, but they would not favor the qualifications that the representatives choosing in imagined ignorance of their own special interests would want to impose. First of all, even when general deterrence has been secured and the possibility of the criminal's repeating his crime is unlikely (e.g., the criminal may have undergone a complete moral conversion), the representatives would still find it legitimate, though maybe not required,[12] to exceed the punishment permitted by the principle in order to deprive the criminal of any benefit from his crime—that is, if it were possible to turn the criminal's punishment to public use, as through forced labor. While the representatives would find this qualification acceptable on the grounds that the criminal could have avoided his fate, a utilitarian would not, since society would not benefit by this arrangement as much as the criminal would by his freedom. Secondly, the representatives would not want to purchase general deterrence at the price of inflicting harsh penalties on only a few offenders. If a considerable number of offenders managed to escape punishment, the representatives would not justify the infliction of punishment sufficient to bring about general deterrence on the few offenders who happened to be apprehended and convicted. Rather, they would choose to take steps to improve the legal system's detection and apprehension procedures; if this could not be done, they would prefer to restrict punishment, even when this would mean less general deterrence and less total utility. Thirdly, although it has been assumed that the laws the criminal violates are reasonably just, once general deterrence has been achieved, the representatives would be inclined for reasons of risk aversion to place limits on the measures to be employed to prevent recidivism that could not be justified in terms of the maximization of utility.[13] Taken together, these qualifications constitute a significant restriction on the pursuit of utilitarian goals with respect to the amount of punishment that may in fairness be inflicted on the criminal for the various crimes he might commit.

Furthermore, as was argued earlier, the representatives would want to impose certain restrictions on the application of punishment that can be captured by the following principle.

> *Principle of Criminal Procedure:* Punishment is to be applied only if 1) safeguards exist to protect the innocent, such as the requirement of conduct, the presumption of innocence, and the evidentiary restrictions of due process, and 2) there are excusing conditions, based on a general requirement of *mens rea.*

While certain restrictions of this sort might also be required for the maximization of utility, the risk aversion of the representatives to choosing principles of retributive justice in imagined ignorance of their own special interests would lead them to interpret the principle as imposing stronger restrictions on the use of punishment than could be justified by utilitarian goals.

These principles, governing the application and the amount of punishment, are the basic principles of a theory of retributive justice that has been shown to be grounded on a standard of justice as fairness which requires that we discount facts of special interest in reaching decisions. By employing an ignorance condition to draw out the implications of this standard, this theory is able to meet the challenge that utilitarians have successfully used to counter most forms of retributivism. It achieves this result by providing a morally defensible account of retributivism that conflicts with the requirements of utility.

4. Opposing Views

JOHN RAWLS' ATTEMPT TO design a decision procedure that captures a commonly accepted ideal of justice as fairness has been widely challenged on various grounds. Nevertheless, critics generally have argued either that Rawls' theory does not present an alternative to existing theories or that is is objectionable on other grounds. In this chapter I propose to consider representative arguments of each of these views. In support of the first view, I will consider R. M. Hare's argument that Rawls' theory has the same practical consequences as the ethical theory Hare developed over a decade ago in *Freedom and Reason*. In support of the second view, I will consider arguments advanced by Robert Nozick to show that Rawls' theory fails to accord with some of our most considered moral judgments and arguments advanced by Marxists to show that Rawls' theory fails to transcend bourgeois liberalism. I hope to show that none of these arguments establishes its case against Rawls' decision procedure.

Hare's Critique

Central to Hare's ethical theory is his account of the logical properties of moral judgments, that is, their universalizability and their prescriptivity.[1] Moral judgments are said to be universalizable in the same sense in which descriptive judgments are universalizable. If I say that something is red or solid, then, according to Hare, I am committed to the view that anything which is like it in the relevant respects would also be red or solid. Similarly, if I say that I ought to imprison A in order to make him pay his debt, then I am committed to the view that others in similar circumstances ought to imprison debtors in order to make them pay their debts. For Hare, a moral judgment is universalizable in the sense that it "logically commits the speaker to making a similar judgment about anything which is exactly like the subject of the original judgment or like it in the relevant respects. The relevant respects are those which formed the grounds of the original judgment." In virtue of their prescriptivity, moral judgments are said to entail imperatives and normally lead to action, from which it follows that, "if a man does what he says he ought not to, though perfectly able to resist the temptation to do it, then there is something wrong with what he says, as well as with what he does." Thus, in Hare's view, a moral judgment not only presupposes a principle (the universalizability requirement), it also leads to action (the prescriptivity requirement).[2]

This explicit account of the logical properties of moral judgments, however, does not reveal all that Hare thinks is built into the ordinary notion of a moral judgment. What else he thinks is implied is best brought out by the examples he uses. Hare asks us to consider the case of a creditor—let us call him Clyde—who is deciding whether he ought to imprison his debtor—whom we can call Dudley—in order to make him pay his debt. Since Clyde is inclined to this course of action, he can assent to the prescription "Let me put Dudley into prison." But to form a moral judgment on the matter, Clyde would have to assent to the principle "Anyone who is in similar circumstances ought to imprison his debtor in order to make him pay his debt." And in virtue of the prescriptivity requirement, this principle would entail "Let Anabel imprison Clyde," where, in the case Hare envisions, Anabel would actually be Clyde's creditor. Consequently, Clyde can only form a moral judgment on the matter if his inclination to imprison Dudley outweighs his disinclination to submit to Anabel's imprisoning him; that is, unless there is a principle that he can assent to which distinguishes his relationship to Dudley from Anabel's relationship to him.

So far, all of this is completely explicable in terms of Hare's account of the universalizability and prescriptivity of moral judgments. But Hare goes on to claim that it isn't necessary that Clyde actually be Anabel's or anyone else's debtor. "[I]t is sufficient that he should consider hypothetically such a case, and see what would be the consequences in it of those moral principles between whose acceptance and rejection he has to decide."[3] Understood in one way, this claim seems perfectly acceptable. After considering hypothetically the case where he is in debt in circumstances exactly similar to those of Dudley, Clyde may decide he cannot form the moral judgment that he ought to imprison Dudley, not because he is in debt to anyone at the moment but because it is probable he will be in debt in the future and, given his disinclination to go to prison, he would not want to commit himself to a moral judgment which in the future is likely to require that he submit to imprisonment. However, this is not the way Hare wants the consideration of hypothethical cases to proceed. Hare imagines Clyde considering hypothetically the case where he is in debt in circumstances exactly similar to those of Dudley and then making his decision by weighing his inclination to imprison Dudley against his own disinclination to submit to imprisonment, all the while disregarding the probability that this hypothetical case will be realized.

But why should Clyde totally disregard the probability of the hypothetical case's ever being realized? If all that one is committed to doing is forming a judgment that is both universalizable and prescriptive, then totally disregarding the probabilities which attach to hypothetical cases is certainly not required. If Clyde, in claiming that he ought to imprison Dudley, is committed to the principle "Anyone who is in similar circumstances ought to imprison his debtor in order to make him pay his debt," to the point of always taking the appropriate action in his own circumstances, then surely he has formed a judgment which is both universalizable and prescriptive, even if he formed his judgment on the basis of the relevant probabilities. To require the consideration of hypothetical cases where roles are reversed in total *disregard of the relevant probabilities* is to impose an additional requirement on moral judgments. Yet Hare does not realize that this requirement is logically distinct from his universalizability and prescriptivity requirements.[4] Rather, he sees it as a logical consequence of those requirements and another way of expressing the fact that, in forming a moral judgment, a person must give equal consideration to the interests of all affected parties. Thus in applying the requirement, a judge is said "to consider, not merely the interests and inclinations of himself and the criminal, but those of all members of society who are affected by his decision."[5]

The requirement to consider hypothetical cases in total disregard of the relevant probabilities, however, is not only logically distinct from Hare's universalizability and prescriptivity requirements, it also does not succeed in characterizing moral judgments as giving equal consideration to the interests of all the affected parties. The reason for this is that in applying the requirement to determine whether A ought to do a certain action affecting B, it is not always logically possible for A to construct a hypothetical case in which he is in B's circumstances, where B's circumstances include such things as ancestry, physical and mental characteristics, and life history. For instance, it is logically impossible for a fanatical Nazi of the sort Hare discusses, who is well informed as to the relevant facts, to imagine himself as having all the characteristics he attributes to Jews while retaining his own personal identity. Since the Nazi's personal identity is linked to having certain physical and mental characteristics and a particular life history, for him to have all the characteristics he attributes to Jews, he would have to be a different person by any acceptable criterion of personal identity. Therefore, in determining whether he ought to persecute Jews, it is logically impossible for a fanatical Nazi to consider a hypothetical case where he has all the characteristics he attributes to Jews. Given that Hare limits the hypothetical cases where roles are reversed to those in which personal identity is preserved ("What *do* you say [*in propria persona*] about a hypothetical case in which you are in the victim's position?"), in certain situations it will be logically impossible for a person forming a moral judgment to imagine himself in the circumstances of those who are affected by his action. For that reason, the requirement to consider hypothetical cases is not sufficient to achieve Hare's purpose of characterizing moral judgments as giving equal consideration to the interests of all the affected parties. It is best, therefore, to view Hare's ethical theory as requiring the following of moral judgments: universalizability, prescriptivity, and equal consideration to the interests of all the affected parties.

Having specified the requirements that Hare's ethical theory places on moral judgments, it is now possible for us to determine in what respects they differ from those that Rawls' theory puts on the choice of principles of justice. Rawls' theory requires that principles of justice be general in form, that is, that they be free from proper names and rigged definite descriptions.[6] This restriction is somewhat stronger than Hare's universalizability requirement, which excludes proper names but permits any type of definite description. Nevertheless, Hare thinks that rigged definite descriptions are excluded by his requirement to consider hypothetical cases where roles are reversed, and while that might not be sufficient for reasons we have just considered, it would appear that such descriptions are excluded by the requirement that moral judgments give equal consideration to the interests of all the affected parties.

In this respect, therefore, Hare's and Rawls' theories do not seem to differ.

To show that Rawls is committed to "some form of prescriptivism," Hare cites a number of passages where Rawls claims that persons in the original position are to assume that the principles they choose will be strictly complied with. However, Rawls makes this claim only to avoid the problems connected with deriving principles of justice for conditions of partial compliance. One cannot infer from it that Rawls thinks that accepting a principle of justice implies strict compliance with that principle. In fact, when discussing civil disobedience, Rawls contends that what justifies such acts is their appeal to a conception of justice that is shared (i.e., accepted) but not fully complied with. Even so, there seems to be a strong enough connection in Rawls' theory between accepting a principle of justice and complying with that principle, so that whatever differences there are between Rawls' theory and Hare's requirement of prescriptivity, they would not appear to result in the choice of different principles of justice. Consequently, if Rawls' theory does not have the same practical consequences as Hare's theory, there must be a significant contrast between Hare's third requirement on moral judgments and Rawls' ideal of justice as fairness.

By requiring that equal consideration be given to the interests of all the affected persons, Hare thinks his ethical theory secures impartiality, fulfilling Bentham's principle "Everyone to count for one, nobody for more than one." Yet this requirement is not considered to be incompatible with sacrificing the interests of many people for the sake of an ideal. In Hare's view, a fanatical Nazi can form a moral judgment, giving equal consideration to the interests of all the affected parties, while prescribing the extermination of the Jews. To do this, he simply has to sincerely judge that the satisfaction of his desire for his Nazi ideal outweighs the dissatisfactions experienced by Jews and others who are affected. Thus a fanatic can form a moral judgment and give equal consideration to the interests of all the affected parties, by being a person "who has some desire whose intensity is such that, even when he gives equal weight to desires of equal intensity, no matter who has them or when, it still preponderates—and who is therefore prepared to universalize fully, over both people and times, the prescription which expressed this desire."[7] Of course, Hare thinks it unlikely that there are fanatics with the requisite preponderate desires and, consequently, that the moral judgments that persons actually do form in circumstances where they are well informed will tend, as a matter of fact, to maximize the net balance of utility without sacrificing people's interests for the sake of any fanatical ideals.

To secure the same impartiality that his own theory requires of moral judgments, Hare assumes, is the purpose of the veil of ignorance in the "simplest and most natural version" of Rawls' decision procedure. Accordingly Hare claims that all that is needed is an "economical veil" of ignorance which only deprives persons in the original position of the knowledge of each person's particular nature and circumstances (including the knowledge of whether they are contemporaries) while giving them complete knowledge of the course of history and the present conditions of society, as well as unlimited general information.[8] Confident that this economical veil is sufficient for impartiality, Hare sees no justification for Rawls' thicker veil of ignorance, which also deprives persons in the original position of knowledge of the course of history and the present conditions of society. An economical veil, Hare thinks, not only secures impartiality but also leads to the choice of the same utilitarian principles as his own ethical theory.

Yet consider the choice facing persons behind Hare's economical veil. Each person is concerned only with advancing his own self-interest, though he is constrained in that pursuit by his ignorance of his own particular nature and circumstances. Without that constraint, he would be able to calculate what best serves his self-interest, faced with only the normal

risks and uncertainties of everyday life. But he must try, behind Hare's economical veil, to determine what is for his best
self-interest when he is faced with the additional uncertainty of
not knowing his own particular nature and circumstances.
This, clearly, requires the choice of principles different from
those he would choose if he were unconstrained by Hare's
economical veil. But would the persons decide that the best
way of advancing their self-interest behind this veil would be
to choose principles which tend to maximize the net balance of
utility in society?

Suppose there are individuals in society who are strongly
committed to fanatical ideals of the sort Hare discusses. Would
persons in the original position consider it in their self-interest
to be committed to principles which require, for that eventual-
ity, the sacrifice of the interests of many people to satisfy those
ideals? Even if the existence of such fanatics is unlikely,
would not the self-interest of each person in the original position still require the choice of principles which protect him
against that possibility? After all, the likelihood of each person's being a fanatic would be very slight when compared with
the likelihood that he would suffer to satisfy someone's fanatical ideal, particularly if the persons in the original position
were to commit themselves to maximizing the net balance of
utility in society. Clearly, then, it is in the self-interest of each
person in the original position to restrict the pursuit of the
maximization of the net balance of utility in society, at least
when this requires the sacrifice of many people's interests for
the sake of fanatical ideals.

This is not an unimportant practical difference between
the requirements Hare puts on moral judgments and his own
version of Rawls' decision procedure. It shows that even a
limited veil of ignorance incorporates an ideal of fairness
which restricts pursuit of the maximization of utility in society,
at least when this requires the sacrifice of many people's interests for the sake of fanatical ideals. Even, so, Rawls' ideal of

justice as fairness is not fully captured by Hare's economical veil of ignorance. Persons behind Hare's economical veil, with their knowledge of the course of history and the present conditions of society, could determine when it was possible to secure considerable utility for the overwhelming majority in society by enslaving or denying basic rights to certain minority groups. They could decide when the possibility of turning up as members of certain disadvantaged minority gruops themselves would be an acceptable risk, in virtue of a high probability of their belonging to the majority.[9] As a result, it would be in the self-interest of the persons behind Hare's economical veil to choose principles which denied the basic needs and desires of certain minorities when this benefited the overwhelming majority in society. In contrast, Rawls' decision procedure firmly guarantees basic rights to minorities. The thicker veil of ignorance in Rawls' theory deprives the persons in the original position of the knowledge that is necessary to assess with confidence the probabilities of their being in particular positions in society, thus making it in the self-interest of each person to secure a high minimum of utility for each person in society. By requiring a high minimum of utility, Rawls' theory safeguards the basic needs and desires of minorities while providing the same restriction against sacrificing the interests of many people for the sake of fanatical ideals as does Hare's version of Rawls' decision procedure.

Nevertheless, it might be argued on Hare's behalf that, assuming uniform declining marginal utility of primary social goods, utilitarian principles would also support a basic minimum of utility for each person in society, and that, with the admitted exception of situations where fanatical ideals are involved, those utilitarian principles would be equivalent to the principles that would be chosen behind Rawls' veil of ignorance.

Yet even this modified version of Hare's claim of practical equivalence cannot be supported. First, as we have seen, the assumption of uniform marginal utility of primary social goods and the other allied assumptions that are needed to approximate the results of justice as fairness are of doubtful validity. Second, we have also seen that, even if one grants these assumptions, persons who are behind Rawls' veil of ignorance would have reason to adopt a somewhat conservative stance, thus choosing principles that secure an even higher minimum of utility at the cost of sacrificing total utility to some degree. Consequently, persons behind Rawls' veil of ignorance could only end up choosing principles which, in this qualified way, are equivalent with utilitarian principles if they are reconstituted either into persons who do not experience any risk aversion whatsoever to entering a one-time gamble that would determine their life prospects and those of their descendants or into "average persons" or a "total person." Yet to modify the restrictions on the original position in either of these ways would simply be a means of ensuring the choice of utilitarian principles. At best, it would simply beg the question as to whether the ideal of justice as fairness is compatible with utilitarian principles. At worst, it would expose an inadequate conception of the nature of persons, which underlies utilitarian principles.

Of course, it does not follow that persons behind Rawls' veil of ignorance would choose principles that required the highest possible minimum for each person in society. Yet what has been shown is that Rawls' decision procedure incorporates an ideal of justice as fairness which, when reflected in either Hare's economical veil of ignorance or more adequately in Rawls' veil of ignorance, results in the choice of principles that significantly differ from the utilitarian principles required by Hare's ethical theory.

Nozick's Critique

If Robert Nozick is correct, however, Rawls' theory has not gone far enough in its rejection of utilitarianism. Regarding Rawls' theory as an undeniable advance over utilitarianism, Nozick objects that the ideal of justice as fairness incorporated into the original position is morally inadequate, conflicting significantly with some of our considered moral judgments.[10] Nor does Nozick's objection take the form of isolated counterexamples to Rawls' theory. Instead, Nozick sketches an alternative theory of distributive justice that has those morally desirable features which he believes Rawls' theory lacks. He calls this theory "an entitlement theory of justice."

According to Nozick's theory, the holdings of persons in society are just if and only if they are entitled to them by certain principles which specify how those holdings came about. There is a "principle of original appropriation," a "principle of transfer," and—for situations where these principles have been violated—a "principle of rectification." The principles of appropriation and transfer are said to contain a Lockean proviso restricting acquisition and exchange so that no one is thereby made worse off; but since the baseline for comparison is so low, the question of the Lockean proviso's being violated arises only in the case of catastrophe.

In Nozick's view, what distinguishes these entitlement principles from other principles of justice, such as the total and average principles of utility and Rawls' two principles of justice, is that these entitlement principles are historical process principles rather than end-state principles; they specify justice in terms of how holdings came about rather than in terms of how holdings are distributed. While admitting that difficulties can be raised with regard to particular historical process principles, Nozick argues that the fundamental problem with Rawls' theory is that his decision procedure is so designed that it is capable of yielding, or seriously entertaining, only end-state principles and never historical process principles of justice. Hence Nozick considers it ill advised to accept Rawls' theory without the certainty that no historical process principles of justice are morally preferable.

To support his claim that Rawls' decision procedure is incapable of yielding or entertaining historical process principles of justice, Nozick asks us to imagine a group of students who have studied for a year, taken examinations, and received grades, though as yet they have not been informed as to what those grades are. We are asked to consider what distribution of grades these students would select using Rawls' decision procedure. Assuming that the sum of all the grades the students would select could not exceed the sum of their actual grades, Nozick thinks the students would favor everyone's getting the same grade, that grade being equal to the sum of their actual grades divided by the number of students. On the other hand, assuming that inequality in the selected grades permitted a variable grade total, Nozick would have us believe the students would be indifferent to whether the higher grades should be given to those most entitled to them or to those least entitled to them, as judged by a qualified impartial observer. Thus whether the grade total is fixed or variable, Nozick concludes, the students would not be led to select an entitlement principle, or any other historical process principle, for the distribution of grades.

Yet the truth of the matter is that students in choosing their grades from behind a veil of ignorance would find it rational to select an entitlement principle of distribution, whether the sum of selected grades were fixed or variable.[11] Using Rawls' decision procedure, the students would discount their knowledge of what their natural and developed abilities are and the extent to which they applied those abilities to their course work in the past or would be willing to do so in the future. Hence, while it would be reasonable for them to secure for themselves at least a certain minimum grade, it would also be in their interest to select a distribution of grades which would not totally frustrate their past and future efforts to achieve higher grades. Even if the principle of distribution selected by the students were to apply only in this one instance of grading, the students would still want the grades to reflect

their past efforts, provided a certain minimum grade was
guaranteed to everyone. Consequently, they would favor an
entitlement principle for the distribution of grades. Moreover,
if the principle to be selected were to apply to future distri-
butions as well, it would be necessary to choose a principle
that would get those students who are motivated by grades to
exert themselves, making possible a higher grade total (where
the grade total was variable) from which everyone would benefit. Only an entitlement principle would achieve that result.
This is not to say that students using Rawls' decision procedure would choose the most morally defensible entitlement
principle to govern the distribution of grades, since their
choice may conflict with the legitimate interests that other
groups (particularly teachers, administrators, and employers)
have in the determination of grades. Nevertheless, the students' own interests would require the choice of some form of
entitlement principle.

It might be objected that the principle that would be
chosen by students using Rawls' decision procedure would be
only a derivative entitlement principle, ultimately to be justified in terms of some end-state principle. More generally,
Nozick might wish to claim that for any entitlement principle
that would be chosen using Rawls' decision procedure, its
justification would always derive from one or more end-state
principles. So understood, Nozick's objection to Rawls'
theory would be that Rawls' decision procedure is incapable of
yielding or even entertaining a nonderivative historical process
conception of justice. Yet Rawls' decision procedure is not
limited to the consideration or purely end-state conceptions of
justice or derivative historical process conceptions of justice.
In fact, when properly understood, the conception of justice
that was derived from Rawls' decision procedure in the previous two chapters is itself a nonderivative historical process
conception of justice.

That this is the case becomes obvious once one realizes

that the principles of distributive and retributive justice that
were derived do not specify how all social goods are to be
distributed, as would an end-state conception of justice. Instead, these principles require only a certain minimum of basic
liberty, opportunity, and economic goods for each person in
society. How goods are distributed above the minimum is
simply a matter of private appropriation and voluntary agreement and exchange. Provided each person's right to a certain
minimum is guaranteed, the results of private appropriation
and voluntary agreement and exchange secure justice whatever
they turn out to be. There is no end-state pattern these results
must satisfy. Nor is each person required to keep the minimum
he is entitled to in a society that conforms to these principles.
He can give up part of it or all of it, or risk losing it for the
chance of gaining a greater share of social goods.[12] The right
to a certain minimum in this Rawlsian conception of justice
functions in the same way as the Lockean proviso does in
Nozick's entitlement conception of justice. For Nozick, the
results of private appropriation and voluntary agreement and
exchange are just, as long as the Lockean proviso against
catastrophe is not violated. Similarly, under this Rawlsian
conception of justice the results of private appropriation and
voluntary agreement and exchange are just so long as the right
to a certain minimum is guaranteed. In neither theory are just
results determined by the satisfaction of some set of end-state
principles of justice, such as the total or average principle of
utility. Consequently, both conceptions are nonderivative historical process conceptions of justice. Accordingly, it is a mistake to think that the fact that Nozick's entitlement principles
represent a nonderivative historical process conception of justice could account for the rejection of those principles by persons using Rawls' decision procedure.

Yet Nozick goes on to raise even more specific objections to Rawls' theory in an effort to account for why his
particular entitlement principles would not be chosen by per-

sons using Rawls' decision procedure.[13] According to Rawls, his decision procedure is explicitly designed to lead to a conception of justice which "nullifies the accidents of natural endowment and the contingencies of social circumstance as counters in quest for political and economic advantage." Rawls justifies structuring this decision procedure this way on the grounds that no one deserves his place in the distribution of native endowments or his initial starting place in society, and that such features are "arbitrary from a moral point of view." Observing that the design of Rawls' decision procedure effectively excludes the choice of his entitlement principles of justice, Nozick argues that the rationale Rawls offers for his decision procedure is inconsistent in at least two respects and, therefore, cannot justify the choices that would be made by persons employing the procedure. In the first place, he claims that Rawls does not completely nullify the role of natural assets in the distribution of social goods but allows them to serve as grounds for providing some persons with larger shares of social goods when this improves the lot of the least advantaged. Secondly, Nozick objects that men's natural assets and initial social circumstances are no more arbitrary from a moral point of view than their rationality or their ability to choose, since all these factors (and many others) are not without moral significance or moral consequences. Both of these objections, however, can be shown to rest upon a misinterpretation of Rawls' theory.

In Rawls' just society, natural endowment and a favorable starting place in society would continue to be assets in the acquisition of social goods, but they would do so in a way that would be acceptable to persons who discounted their knowledge of their own particular natural and social assets, that is, persons using Rawls' decision procedure. How these factors counted as assets, therefore, would accord with the preferences of persons who were not partial to those favored by natural and social assets, since persons using Rawls' decision procedure would have no reason to think that such a policy would benefit them. Thus the sense in which Rawls' decision procedure leads to a conception of justice that nullifies the accidents of natural endowment and the contingencies of social circumstance as counters in the quest for political and economic advantage is one of degree; that is, it leads to a conception of justice which only nullifies these factors as *partial* counters in the quest for political and economic advantage. Interpreted in this way, the rationale Rawls offers for his decision procedure is not inconsistent, as Nozick charged, with allowing natural assets to serve as the basis for giving some persons larger shares of social goods when this improves the lot of the least advantaged.   *207764*

Moreover, in claiming that these factors are arbitrary from a moral point of view, Rawls is not denying Nozick's point that these factors, and many others, have moral significance and moral consequences. In Rawls' just society, favorable natural assets and the contingencies of social circumstance function to produce moral consequences that are fair and impartial. To say that such factors are arbitrary from a moral point of view is just another way that Rawls has of claiming that no one deserves his natural assets or initial starting place in society. Since these factors are not deserved, then, in Rawls' view, they should not serve as partial counters in the quest for political and economic advantage. If these factors were deserved, then presumably Rawls would maintain that there would be grounds for partiality. While Nozick never claims that anyone deserves his natural assets, he holds that a person is entitled to them. This entitlement, however, would no more justify a lifting of the veil of ignorance with respect to natural and social assets to guarantee the choice of morally acceptable principles of distributive justice than a person's right not to be subject to cruel and inhumane punishment would justify a lifting of the veil of ignorance with respect to whether the person is criminally inclined or has committed a

serious offense in order to guarantee the choice of morally
acceptable principles of retributive justice. Since Nozick provides no other ground for partiality, I conclude that his arguments against Rawls' theory do not succeed in showing that
the ideal of justice as fairness, captured by Rawls' decision
procedure, offends against our considered moral judgments.

The Marxist Critique

Turning to the Marxist critique of Rawls' theory, we find
two distinct objections. The first grants that a conception of
justice would be chosen by persons using Rawls' decision
procedure, but then contends the conception which would be
chosen is simply that of bourgeois liberalism, while the second
denies that any conception of justice would be chosen if persons using Rawls' decision procedure were aware of the general
facts of class conflict.

According to the first objective, Rawls' decision procedure simply captures a conception of bourgeois liberalism. In
support of this objection, two arguments are usually presented.
First, it is argued that the principles of social cooperation that
would be chosen are principles that interfere least with the
realization of self-interest rather than principles that are directed at promoting the welfare of others.[14] Second, it is argued that the inadequate character of the principles that would
be chosen is further brought out by the fact that socializing the
means of production is not a necessary requirement of the
principles that would be chosen.[15]

The first argument, however, rests in part on a confusion
between the reasons persons would have for accepting principles of distributive and retributive justice when constrained
and when not constrained by Rawls' decision procedure. Were
persons constrained by Rawls' decision procedure, they would
choose or accept principles of justice for reasons of self-

interest, since they are seeking to further their own self-interest as best they can under the ignorance conditions imposed by the decision procedure. Thus, imagining themselves to be ignorant of their own special interests, they would be led by reasons of self-interest to choose the principles in Chapters 2 and 3. However, were persons unconstrained by Rawls' decision procedure, they would normally not be led by reasons of self-interest to accept those same principles. Rather, they would accept such principles only if they were genuinely motivated by reasons of concern for the welfare of others. Thus for persons who are unconstrained by Rawls' decision procedure, accepting the principles of distributive and retributive justice in Chapters 2 and 3 implies a genuine concern for the welfare of others.

Moreover, this concern for the welfare of others is not derived from a concern for one's own welfare but is based on an equal concern for the basic needs of each and every person. Consequently, a society in which virtually everyone is motivated by such a concern to comply with the principles in Chapters 2 and 3 would not be unlike Marx's ideal society in which each person would be free to creatively express himself in his labor and have the enjoyment of knowing that part of the product of his labor would satisfy someone else's needs.[16]

The second argument in support of the first Marxist objection, however, is not so easy to counter, for it must be admitted that a social contract theory that utilizes a Rawlsian veil of ignorance does not necessarily require socialization of the means of production. In *A Theory of Justice,* Rawls does not deny that socialization may *sometimes* be required. Rather, he claims that whether it is required or not depends on the particular historical circumstances of a society. Yet even if socializing the means of production is not a necessary requirement of the principles of justice that are derived from Rawls' decision procedure, it does not follow that Rawls' decision procedure only succeeds in capturing a conception of bourgeois liberalism. Actually, for persons who accept the principles of justice in Chapters 2 and 3, the question of whether or not to socialize the means of production may not be as momentous as it seems. For in order for a system of private ownership of the means of production to satisfy the high minimum requirements of those principles, it may be necessary to limit and redistribute private holdings to such a degree that the ownership of all the major means of production would, as a result, be widely dispersed throughout the society. As Marx pointed out, the widespread exploitation of laborers, associated with early capitalism, only began when large numbers "had been robbed of all their own means of production and of all the guarantees of existence afforded by the old feudal system" by persons and economic groups who already had considerable wealth and power.[17] But the concentration of wealth and power that is necessary to carry out such exploitation is not likely to be found in a society which, in accordance with the principles in Chapters 2 and 3, provides for the basic needs of all its members as well as for the basic needs of distant peoples and future generations. Consequently, a shift from such restricted private ownership of the means of production to socialization of those means may have little practical consequence.

According to the second and more serious objection to Rawls' theory, persons using Rawls' decision procedure will not even be able to choose a conception of justice if they are aware of the general facts of class conflict. Thus it is claimed that if persons using Rawls' decision procedure are aware of such facts, they will know that members of different classes have diametrically opposed interests and needs. As a consequence, social arrangements that are acceptable to members of one class, say the capitalist class, would be quite unacceptable to members of an opposing class, that is, the proletariat class. Accordingly, if persons know that conflicts between opposing classes cannot be resolved without leaving members of one or the other group extremely dissatisfied with the result, they will not be able to derive principles of justice when using Rawls' decision procedure.[18]

To understand the force of this objection, it is necessary to be clear about the various ways in which people's needs and interests can be related in a society. One possibility is that the needs and interests of different members of a society are, in fact, perfectly complementary. If that were the case, there would be little difficulty designing a social arrangement that would be acceptable to every member. Nor would Rawls' decision procedure be needed to design a fair solution. In such a society, no conflicts at all would arise as long as each person acted in his overall self-interest.

A second possibility is that the needs and interests of different members of a society are in moderate conflict. In deriving his two principles of justice, Rawls actually limits himself to a consideration of social conditions where only moderate conflict obtains. For such conditions, it seems clear that Rawls' decision procedure could be usefully employed to design a fair social arrangement. Moreover, in a society in which the needs and interests of different members were only in moderate conflict, it should not be that difficult to secure compliance with the principles of conflict resolution that would be selected by Rawls' decision procedure. Consequently, persons using Rawls' decision procedure would know that the members of such a society, when aided by a minimal enforcement system, would be able to abide by whatever principles they were to select.

A third possibility is that the needs and interests of the different members of a society are in extreme conflict, and that the conflict has the form that Marx calls "class conflict." Let us consider the case in which the opposing classes are the capitalist class and the proletariat class. No doubt persons using Rawls' decision procedure would know that, in such a society, compliance with almost any principles of conflict resolution could be achieved only by means of a stringent enforcement system. But why should that fact keep them from choosing any principles of social cooperation whatsoever? Surely persons using Rawls' decision procedure would still have grounds to provide for the basic needs of the members of the proletariat class and, thus, would be inclined to favor the principles of justice in Chapters 2 and 3. However, would they not also have reason to temper the sacrifice to be imposed on the members of the capitalist class, knowing, as they do, how much less prosperous and satisfied the members of that class would be under the principles of justice in Chapters 2 and 3? But if considerations of this latter sort could serve as reasons for persons using Rawls' decision procedure, the first Marxist objection to Rawls' theory would clearly apply, for it could be argued that the principles of social cooperation that would be subsequently derived would not be a morally adequate conception of justice. A morally adequate conception of justice, it could be argued, would not provide grounds for tempering the sacrifice to be imposed on the members of the capitalist class.

Fortunately for social contract theory, it is possible to show that consideration favoring tempering the sacrifice of the members of the capitalist class would not serve as reasons for persons using Rawls' decision procedure. This is because persons using Rawls' decision procedure and imagining themselves to be ignorant of whether they belong to the capitalist or the proletariat class would have grounds to discount such considerations in deciding upon principles of social cooperation. They would realize that members of the capitalist class would have a status analogous to that of criminals who have taken goods that rightfully belong to others. For the members of the capitalist class are not ''compelled'' to pursue their interest by depriving the members of the proletariat class of an acceptable minimum of social goods. They act as they do, in violation of the principles of justice in Chapters 2 and 3, simply to acquire more social goods for themselves. Unlike members of the proletariat class, members of the capitalist class could be reasonably expected to act otherwise. On this account, persons using Rawls' decision procedure would judge that if anyone were required to make sacrifices during the transition to a society that accorded with the principles in Chapters 2 and 3, it would have to be the members of the capitalist class, for only they could be reasonably expected to have acted differently in the past. Of course, if there is any question of diminished responsibility, persons using Rawls' decision procedure would want to deal with the matter in a manner analogous to the way it would be considered in criminal cases. Thus it seems clear that the second Marxist objection to Rawls' decision procedure is also mistaken.

Obviously, the fact that the critiques of Rawls' decision procedure offered by Hare, Nozick, and various Marxists all proved unsuccessful does not suffice to show that some other critique might not succeed. Nevertheless, given the representative character of the critiques that have failed, there would appear to be a strong presumptive case in favor of Rawls' decision procedure. In the next chapter, further confirmation is provided by showing that there is a role for Rawls' decision procedure even if we begin with the libertarian's ideal of liberty.

5. Neo-Libertarianism

LIBERTARIANS LIKE TO THINK of themselves as defenders of liberty. F. A. Hayek, for example, sees his work as restating an ideal of liberty for our times. "We are concerned," says Hayek, "with that condition of men in which coercion of some by others is reduced as much as possible in society."[1] Similarly, John Hospers believes that libertarianism is "a philosophy of personal liberty—the liberty of each person to live according to his own choices, provided that he does not attempt to coerce others and thus prevent them from living according to their choices."[2] And Robert Nozick claims that if a conception of justice goes beyond libertarian "side-constraints," it cannot avoid the prospect of continually interfering with people's lives.

Taking liberty to be the absence of interference by other persons, libertarians generally agree that liberty only justifies a minimal or night-watchman state. According to Nozick,

> Our main conclusions about the state are that a minimal state, limited to the narrow functions of protecting against force, theft, fraud, enforcement of contracts, and so on, is justified; that any more extensive state will violate persons' rights not to be forced to do certain things, and is unjustified; and that the minimal state is inspiring as well as right.[3]

Libertarians hold that while other social ideals, such as equality and humanitarianism, if shown to be acceptable and

106

of sufficient priority, may well justify a more extensive state, liberty never does. Or more precisely, they maintain that an ideal of liberty cannot be used to justify anything more extensive than a night-watchman state as long as liberty is understood "negatively," as the absence of interference or coercion by other persons, rather than "positively," as the presence of a particular activity or ability.

In what follows I shall argue that this commonly accepted libertarian view is mistaken. I shall show that moral commitment to an ideal of "negative" liberty does not lead to a night-watchman state but, instead, requires sufficient government to provide each person in society with the relatively high minimum of liberty that persons using Rawls' decision procedure would select. The political program that is justified by an ideal of negative liberty I shall call "neo-libertarianism."

The Argument for the Night-Watchman State

The libertarian argument for the night-watchman state begins with the acceptable premise that voluntary agreements represent an ultimate ideal for social interaction. This ideal, libertarians contend, finds its fullest expression in a market economy, where buyers and sellers, employers and employees voluntarily agree to exchange the goods they possess. Thus it is assumed that the requirements for voluntary agreements between persons with unequal resources are easily satisfied in a market economy. As long as alternative contractual arrangements make it possible for buyers and sellers and employers and employees to "take their business elsewhere," libertarians believe that agreements that are reached in market transactions are completely voluntary. On these grounds, libertarians claim that the only significant role left for the state is to prevent and to rectify departures from a market economy resulting from fraud, theft, or the use of force. Any more extensive role for the state, they contend, would restrict people's liberty; that is to say, it would restrict liberty understood negatively, as the absence of interference by other persons. Accordingly, libertarians conclude that only a night-watchman state can be justified in terms of an ideal of negative liberty.

The libertarian argument for the night-watchman state also seeks to show that other social ideals cannot justify a more extensive state. Libertarians either maintain that other social ideals, purporting to justify a more extensive state, are without justification or they claim that these social ideals have lower priority when compared with the ideal of negative liberty. But there is not always agreement as to which critical approach is appropriate. Thus with respect to an ideal of equality, Nozick and Hayek adopt different approaches: Nozick maintains that an ideal of equality has not been effectively justified, while Hayek maintains that the ideal has some validity but that negative liberty is the superior ideal. Allowing for such disagreements, both critical approaches could also be used by libertarians against various conceptions of positive liberty.

One conception of positive liberty, usually associated with Jean Jacques Rousseau and G. W. F. Hegel but also found in the works of John Locke and John Stuart Mill, defines liberty in terms of the presence of a certain activity—the activity of doing what one ought. Locke, for example, uses this conception to define liberty in the state of nature. "The Natural Liberty of Man," Locke says, "is to have only the Law of Nature for his Rule." Since the "Law of Nature" for Locke is a moral law, it follows that having only the "Law of Nature" for one's rule or principle of action would always entail doing what one ought to do. On other occasions, Locke uses this conception of positive liberty to distinguish liberty from license. License is understood as the activity of doing what one ought not do; liberty is understood as the activity of doing what one ought to do. Thus, for example, contemporary defenders of this conception of liberty would identify license with the selling of pornography or the promotion of prostitution or gambling. This conception of positive liberty is also the source of Rousseau's paradoxical claim that persons who refuse to obey the General Will should be "forced to be free." For the paradox of how persons can be free and forced at the same time is resolved if "freedom" means the activity of doing what one ought to do, since it is certainly possible to force people to do what they ought to do.

This conception of positive liberty (libertarians would have to admit) has some validity as a social ideal. An ideal requiring people to do what they ought to do cannot be all bad. Nevertheless, libertarians could argue that this ideal of positive liberty will not serve to justify a more extensive state. As Rousseau's paradoxical claim suggests, a state can guarantee its citizens complete liberty in this sense while still exercising whatever force is necessary to make them always do what they ought to do. Complete liberty, in this sense, is clearly compatible with the total enforcement of all aspects of morality. Consequently, this ideal of liberty could suffice to justify a more extensive state only if one could defend the view that people should always be prevented from doing what they ought not to do. But even Lord Devlin, a strong advocate of the enforcement of morality, would find this view too extreme. What is required, therefore, is a standard for determining the extent to which morality should be enforced, a standard that is not provided for by this ideal of liberty.

More promising is the conception of positive liberty that defines liberty in terms of the presence of a certain ability—the ability to do whatever one might conceivably want. One advantage of this conception of positive liberty over the previous conception is that it cannot be used to claim that forcing a person to do what he ought to do thereby increases his liberty. If forcing a person to do what he ought to do increases anyone's liberty, as determined by this ideal, it ordinarily increases the liberty of others who benefit from the person's doing what he ought; only in paternalistic practices would it be possible to increase the liberty of the person who is actually forced to do what he ought to do. Another advantage of this conception of liberty is that it does not make liberty depend solely on what a person actually happens to want. If liberty were specified solely in terms of the ability to do what one actually wants, it would be possible to increase a person's liberty by restricting his actual wants through social conditioning. Thus a government could increase the liberty of its citizens by socially conditioning them always to favor its policies. A person could also increase his own liberty by a process of self-denial that extinguished wants he was unable to satisfy. However, liberty that could always be increased in this fashion would be a somewhat questionable ideal. Since the value of having the ability to do whatever one actually wants is enhanced to the extent that one also has the ability to do whatever one might conceivably want, liberty defined in terms of this more general ability is clearly the more desirable ideal.

Yet it is obviously impossible for everyone in society to be guaranteed complete liberty as defined by this ideal; after all, people's actual wants, as well as their conceivable wants, can come into serious conflict. In this respect, however, this conception of positive liberty is no worse than the conception of negative liberty that is defended by libertarians. Given people's actual and conceivable wants, it is also impossible for everyone in society to be completely free from the interference of other persons.

The main difficulty with this conception of positive liberty is that it identifies inability with lack of liberty, thereby construing liberties too broadly to satisfy the requirements of a social ideal. According to this conception, a person who is unable to vote, due to legal restrictions, and a person who is unable to run a mile, due to advanced age, would *both* be lacking in liberty. Yet it seems plausible to claim that for liberty to be a *social ideal,* it must be possible to assign moral responsibility for any lack of liberty. This means that for liberty to be a social ideal, an aged person's inability to run a mile cannot be regarded (except in rare circumstances) as a lack of liberty; consequently, only an inability like that of a person restricted by law from voting—an inability for which other persons are morally responsible by their interference—can ordinarily be regarded as a lack of liberty. Thus by defining a lack of liberty so broadly as to include all human inabilities, this conception of positive liberty ignores the requirement for assigning responsibility that is implicit in a social ideal.

Assuming that one rejects this conception of positive liberty, is it necessary to go further and adopt the libertarian view that liberty is a negative social ideal? Arguing against this view, Gerald MacCallum claims that every ideal of liberty has both its negative ("freedom from") and positive ("freedom to") aspects. Actually, MacCallum contends that whenever the freedom of agents is in question there is always a triadic relation implying the freedom of something (an agent or agents) from something, to do or become (or not do or not become) something.[4] Yet it is possible to accept MacCallum's thesis and still maintain that liberty functions primarily as a negative social ideal. One could argue that although we can always specify what it is to have complete liberty negatively in terms of a person's being totally free from the interference or coercion of other persons, if we tried to specify what it is to have complete liberty positively in terms of what a person is free to do or become (or not do or not become), we would have to provide a variety of different accounts for different persons and for different circumstances—an extremely difficult, if not impossible, task. One could, of course, say that to have complete liberty positively is to be completely free to lead one's life. Yet if liberty, so conceived, is to be a social ideal, it cannot exclude every constraint or obstacle to leading one's life. Rather, it can only exclude those constraints or obstacles that result from the interference of other persons, that is, those resulting from the lack of negative liberty. This would seem to provide some justification for the libertarian view that liberty, understood negatively, is the more basic social ideal.

The Ideal of Negative Liberty

The libertarian argument for the night-watchman state is clearly strongest when it is directed against various conceptions of positive liberty and other social ideals such as equality and humanitarianism. The argument is weakest when it assesses the implications of the libertarian's own social ideal of negative liberty. Libertarians are quite capable of enumerating a variety of ways in which governments deprive people of their liberty; thus it is said that governments restrict people's liberty by tariffs, taxes, wage and price regulations, credit restrictions, public monopolies, public work projects, and various welfare programs such as social security and health care. For the most part, these practices are thought to restrict people's liberty in undesirable ways. Commenting on social security programs, Hospers says:

> If I were given a choice, I would say, "No thanks" to social security: "I have found much better ways of saving for my old age than by subscribing to the government program"—or I might not want to save at all, or to stake everything on a business enterprise that requires my entire capital outlay *now*. But I am not given this choice: the government says, "You have to pay into this whether you like it or not."[5]

Nozick even goes so far as to claim that taxation of earnings from labor is on a par with forced labor; yet libertarians are not similarly sensitive to the loss of liberty that occurs in the market place. When an employer decides to lay someone off, for example, Hospers claims the employer is simply deciding against continuing a voluntary exchange and is not restricting the person's liberty. Likewise, Hayek claims that as long as workers who are laid off can find alternative employment, their liberty is not being restricted. But how can requiring a person to pay $500 into a social security program, under threat of greater financial loss, infringe upon the person's liberty when requiring a person to take a job that pays $500 less, under threat of greater financial loss, does not infringe upon the person's liberty? Surely, it would seem that if one requirement restricts a person's liberty, the other will also.

To distinguish these cases, some libertarians claim that only intentional interference by others restricts a person's liberty. Requiring a person to pay $500 into a social security program under threat of greater financial loss, they contend, is intentional interference by others and hence restricts the person's liberty, while requiring a person to take a job that pays $500 less, under a similar threat, is but the unintended result of individuals' trying to better themselves in a market economy and hence does not restrict the person's liberty. But whether interference with a person's life is intentional or not is relevant only in determining the extent to which others are responsible for that interference. Although people clearly are more responsible for actions they do intentionally, they can still be responsible for actions they do unintentionally, especially if they were morally negligent and should have foreseen the consequences of their actions. Since moral responsibility can extend to both intentional and unintentional interference with a person's life, there seems to be no reason for not considering both types of interference to be restrictions of a person's liberty. What is crucial to liberty as a social ideal is whether people are morally responsible for interfering with a person's life, irrespective of whether that interference is intentional or not.

While granting that unintentional as well as intentional interference can restrict a person's liberty, W. A. Parent has recently argued that not every interference with a person's life for which others are morally responsible is a restriction of liberty.[6] In fact, Parent would not regard either of the two previous cases as a restriction of liberty. Each case would be said to violate a self-evident principle, to wit: a person cannot be socially unfree to do what he can do or has already done. For a person can refuse to contribute to a required social security program, even when faced with a greater financial loss, and he can refuse to take a lower-paying job, even when faced with a comparable loss. Hence Parent would conclude, from applying his principle, that in neither case is the person socially unfree; that is, in neither case is the interference with the person's life a restriction of liberty.

Parent's principle is certainly a reasonable requirement for an ideal of liberty. Parent simply misapplies it. When correctly applied, the principle has the consequence that every interference with a person's life for which others are morally responsible is a restriction of liberty. What Parent fails to see is that in every such case of interference there is always some action the person can no longer perform as a result of that interference. The person who is faced with greater financial loss if he refuses to pay $500 into a social security program cannot perform the action of refusing-to-pay-into-the-program-without-the-imminent-risk-of-a-greater-financial-loss. Interference by the state makes it impossible for the person to perform that action. Again, in the second case, the intentional interference with the person's life, resulting from market transactions, makes it impossible for him to perform the action of refusing-to-take-a-lower-paying-job-without-incurring-the-imminent-risk-of-greater-financial-loss. In short, in both cases there is an action the person cannot perform because of the interference of other persons. And it is that action which the person is socially unfree to do. Thus, in both cases, Parent's principle is satisfied. In general, therefore, when we speak of a person's liberty being restricted by the laws of the state, this implies not that it is impossible for the person to violate those laws but rather that it is impossible for the person to perform the action of violating-the-laws-of-the-state-without-incurring-some-risk-of-punishment-or-penalty.

So far it has been argued that any intentional or unintentional interference with a person's life for which other persons are morally responsible is a restriction of liberty. Disagreement can arise, however, over what constitutes an interference with a person's life. If a sick person is simply left alone and dies for lack of treatment, for example, has his liberty been restricted? Or is a person's liberty restricted if he is left alone to starve to death? Put more generally, can acts of omission as well as acts of commission interfere with a person's life? The importance of this question derives from the fact that libertarians believe that interference requires an act of commission, from which they think it follows that it is impossible to justify the practices of a welfare state in terms of an ideal of negative liberty.

No doubt in standard cases the interference which restricts a person's liberty results from an act of commission. A prisoner's liberty, for example, is restricted by what his jailers do rather than by what they refrain from doing. Of course, a prisoner could regain his liberty if his jailers gave him the keys and turned their backs, but the omitted acts are certainly not causally sufficient to restrict the prisoner's liberty. If these omitted acts restrict the prisoner's liberty at all, they do so only in virtue of the coercive actions already performed by the jailers.

But suppose a person were starving to death and the only causally relevant actions for which others were morally responsible were actions of failing to give him the food he needs. Would those acts of omission interfere with the person's life? C. B. Macpherson believes they would. For Macpherson, any humanly alterable condition that prevents a person from doing something either directly or indirectly interfers with that person's life and, hence, restricts his liberty.[7] No doubt, construing interference in this fashion would make it possible to defend the practices of a welfare state in terms of an ideal of negative liberty, but it would not win many converts among libertarians. Libertarians would think that Macpherson's interpretation simply begs the question of whether acts of omission interfere with a person's life.

Yet it is possible to grant libertarians that interference with a person's life requires an act of commission and still maintain that liberty is restricted when people in need are simply left alone. In the first place, most people would be able to take from others the goods and resources they need if they were not prohibited from doing so by those who possess the goods and resources. Such prohibitions would obviously be acts of commission that interfere with people's lives and, hence, restrict their liberty. Secondly, with respect to persons who are in such dire need that they cannot even take from others the goods and resources they need, restrictions of liberty will also arise if there are other persons who are interested in transferring goods and resources to them but are prohibited from doing so by some of those who possess the goods and resources. Consequently, in virtually every case in which people in need are left alone to care for themselves their liberty and/or the liberty of others is actually restricted. For this reason, even if one accepts the libertarian view that interference with a person's life requires an act of commission, it still may be possible to justify the practices of a welfare state in terms of an ideal of negative liberty.

From what has been argued, it is apparent that restrictions of liberty are more pervasive than libertarians are usually willing to admit. In fact, attempting a more general account, it seems plausible to claim that *any intentional or unintentional act of commission for which others are morally responsible interferes with a person's life and thereby restricts his liberty if that act prevents him from doing something he could otherwise do*.

And in accordance with Parent's principle that a person

cannot be socially unfree to do what he can do or has already done, we could add that *if a person's action prevents another from doing some action he could otherwise do, then the person's action renders it impossible for the other person to perform that action.*

Of course, some libertarians may object to this account on the grounds that to interfere with a person's life so as to restrict his liberty, one must violate his rights.[8] Thus it may be claimed that in the social security example, where a person is required to pay $500 under threat of a greater financial loss, the person's liberty is being restricted because his rights to his justly acquired possessions are being violated, whereas in the employment example, where a person is required to take a job that pays $500 less, under threat of a greater financial loss, the person's liberty is not being restricted since his rights are not being violated, presumably because he has no right to a higher-paying job. But to define liberty in this fashion would make liberty a derivative social ideal. Whether a person's liberty is being restricted would thus depend on what a person's right are at any given moment. This would have the odd consequence that if we were to justly imprison someone for committing a crime, we would not be restricting his liberty because he would have forfeited his right to live his life as he pleases. Likewise, it could turn out that in a society in which people voluntarily contracted into extensive paternalistic practices, there may be no more restriction of liberty, understood as the nonviolation of people's rights, than in the most individualistic society, even though it would seem that the reason people have for contracting into paternalistic practices (from Christmas clubs to monastic orders) is to restrict their liberty for some good purpose. Thus while it must be granted that people's rights should determine how much liberty they should have at any given time, if liberty is to serve as an ultimate social ideal for libertarians, then it must be specified in a manner similar to the account just proposed.

According to that account, restrictions of liberty can be

quite severe (like forcing a person to give over all his possessions at gunpoint) or they can be very slight and even trivial
(like accidentally stepping on a person's toe). The relative
significance of a restriction of liberty depends upon the relative
significance of the action(s) prevented by that restriction. Significant restrictions of liberty can be imposed either by the
government (like a steeply progressive income tax) or by private individuals and groups (like dehumanizing work conditions in a market economy). Significant restrictions of liberty
are called "coercive" when they prevent a person from doing
something he could otherwise do, either by applying considerable physical force or by threatening some highly undesirable
consequence. Although libertarians are quick to point out that
significant restrictions of liberty by the government are greater
under a more extensive state than under a night-watchman
state, they are slow to see that significant restrictions of liberty
by private individuals and groups can also be greater under a
night-watchman state than under a more extensive state. Given
the practical impossibility of avoiding all restrictions of liberty, the crucial question for the advocate of negative liberty
is: In what ways should liberty be restricted? What is needed,
therefore, is an acceptable procedure for deciding upon principles for restricting liberty in society. The libertarian's hope is
that from such a procedure it is possible to derive principles
that justify a night-watchman state.

A Rawlsian Decision Procedure

In keeping with the libertarian's concern for negative
liberty, we might consider the possibility of determining principles for restricting liberty by having a meeting of all the
members of a society. Such a meeting (assuming it practically
possible) might result in a greater appreciation of all the relevant viewpoints—if, that is, each member were given a chance

to argue in favor of his or her particular interests. However, it is unrealistic to think that the persons at this meeting would be able to reach a unanimous agreement with respect to principles for restricting liberty. As we have noted before, the chances of that occurring would be very slight, unless the members had some procedure for compromising their particular interests.

Suppose, then, that the members of this society were to adopt a procedure analogous to the one proposed in Chapters 2 and 3. Suppose, that is to say, that the members of this society, in deciding upon principles for restricting liberty, were to discount the knowledge of which particular interests happen to be their own. Although they would actually know what their own particular interests were, they would not take that knowledge into account when selecting principles for restricting liberty. In selecting such principles, they would reason from their knowledge of all the particular interests in their society but not from their knowledge of which particular interests happen to be their own.[9] In employing this decision procedure, the members of this society (like judges who discount prejudicial information in order to reach fair decisions) would be able to give a fair hearing to everyone's particular interests. If we further assume that the members were well informed of all the particular interests in their society and were fully capable of rationally deliberating with respect to that information, their deliberations would culminate in a unanimous decision. This is because each of them would be deliberating in a rationally correct manner with respect to the same information and would be using a decision procedure that led to a uniform evaluation of the alternatives; consequently, each would favor the same principles for restricting liberty in society. Given that the principles that would be selected by this procedure would result from a unanimous agreement in which everyone's particular interests received a fair hearing, there seem to be no reasonable grounds for libertarians to object to the principles that would be derived.

But *what* principles would be derived from this procedure? In previous chapters it was argued that persons employing an analogous decision procedure (in which they assume ignorance of their own particular interests) would have reason to reject both maximin and utilitarian principles of justice. Maximin principles, by ignoring the relevance of tradeoffs between parties at different levels of welfare (e.g., tradeoffs between the Free Riders and Hard Toilers), require a minimum of social goods that would be regarded as too high by persons using this decision procedure, while utilitarian principles, by focusing their concern on either ''average persons'' or a ''total person,'' could require a minimum of social goods that would be regarded as too low. Thus persons using this decision procedure would want to specify the minimum of social goods so as to compromise the requirements of both types of principles. Since it was argued in Chapter 2 that this could be done by specifying the minimum of social goods in terms of a person's basic needs, there is no reason why this same minimum, understood as a minimum of liberty, could not also be specified in terms of a person's basic needs. Thus we could define an acceptable minimum of liberty as the liberty necessary to meet the normal costs of satisfying the basic needs of a person in the society in which he lives. Determined in this way, a minimum of liberty would enable a person to acquire the goods and resources necessary for satisfying his basic needs. Other liberties would enable a person to transfer goods and resources, not necessarily his own, to provide for the basic needs of others. Persons using this decision procedure would want liberties of both types to ensure equal consideration for everyone's basic needs.

Of course, the exact minimum of liberty that persons using this decision procedure would require necessarily depends upon the particular economic and social resources available in a society. Yet whatever the acceptable minimum of liberty for a particular society, how social goods are to be distributed above the minimum would simply be a matter of private appropriation and voluntary agreement and exchange. Provided each person is guaranteed the acceptable minimum of liberty, persons using this decision procedure would have little reason to object to the results of private appropriation and voluntary agreement and exchange. For example, people could voluntarily agree to set up various forms of government for themselves, from direct democracies to dictatorships, as long as the right to the acceptable minimum of liberty were respected. Nor would each person be required to keep the minimum of liberty he is guaranteed; a person could give up part or all of it, or risk losing it for the chance of gaining a greater share of liberties or other social goods.[10] Thus the most general principle of neo-libertarianism is the following:

> *Needs and Agreement Principle:* The results of private appropriation and voluntary agreement and exchange are morally justified provided each person is guaranteed the liberty that is necessary to meet the normal costs of satisfying his basic needs in the society in which he lives.[11]

In neo-libertarianism, the right to an acceptable minimum of liberty functions in the same way as the Lockean proviso does in Nozick's libertarianism. According to Nozick's view, the results of voluntary agreement and private appropriation are morally justified so long as the Lockean proviso against catastrophe is not violated. Similarly, in neo-libertarianism, the results of voluntary agreement and private appropriation are morally justified so long as the right to an acceptable minimum of liberty is guaranteed. Only with respect to the minimum of liberty it requires does neo-libertarianism differ significantly from Nozick's libertarianism.

It may be objected, however, that to require a high minimum of liberty is a significant difference, since most libertarians would definitely oppose such a minimum on the grounds that it would conflict with a person's right to acquire property. But while guaranteeing such a minimum of liberty would certainly place some restriction on a person's right to acquire property over and above what is necessary to satisfy his basic needs, why should a person's right to acquire property take precedence over guaranteeing that minimum?

Surely we cannot expect that people will universally consent to a lower minimum of liberty so as to have a greater opportunity to acquire property. After all, a minimum that provides each person with the liberty that is necessary to satisfy his or her basic needs would be quite attractive to many people.

It may be claimed, of course, that property rights can legitimately arise by some Lockean process of creatively "mixing" one's labor with previously unowned goods or by the voluntary transfer of goods that have been subjected to such a Lockean process. But whether a person can come to have property rights through these processes of acquisition and transfer will depend on whether others can rightfully interfere with such processes and, if others can rightfully interfere, on whether they have forfeited their rights to do so.

For example, let us assume that I can acquire property rights to a piece of unowned land by creatively mixing my labor with the land and that the piece of land is more than I really need to satisfy my basic needs. Could others rightfully appropriate that part of it that I did not require for my basic needs if no other means of satisfying their basic needs were available? Surely others could not be morally required to do nothing to avoid seriously endangering their health and sanity just because I have already creatively mixed my labor with all the available resources for satisfying their basic needs. Therefore, persons in such dire need, or their agents, would seem to be within their rights to appropriate the surplus goods I possess, unless they have forfeited their rights to an adequate minimum of liberty (e.g., by squandering their possessions or by gambling away their rights to an adequate minimum of liberty for the chance of acquiring greater possessions and thereby greater liberty).

No doubt it will frequently be possible to prevent persons in dire need, or their agents, from interfering with processes of appropriation and transfer, but this does not mean that it would be right to do so. Since a moral solution to the conflict between persons who possess surplus goods and persons who are in dire need would have to be one each party could accept as reasonable, such a solution could not demand that persons in dire need renounce the only available means they have at their command for satisfying their basic needs. Although providing an adequate minimum of liberty is certainly not a productive exchange between persons who possess surplus goods and persons who are in dire need, since each party would presumably be better off if the other did not exist, nevertheless, providing such a minimum is certainly the only reasonable solution if both parties are presumed to have the right to exist. Furthermore, a person's right to an adequate minimum of liberty would not be unconditional, but would apply to the surplus goods of others only when there is no other means at the person's command for satisfying his basic needs.

Yet libertarians sometimes argue that persons who are in need would be better off in a society that did not guarantee as high a minimum as is required by the Needs and Agreement Principle. In a society that did not guarantee a high minimum, it is claimed, persons would be more productive because they would be able to keep more of what they produced, and with this greater productivity, it is claimed, persons in need would benefit even more from private charity than they would from having as high a minimum as that required by the Needs and Agreement Principle. But it is certainly doubtful that this would occur, because it would only make sense to secure the minimum of the Needs and Agreement Principle in a manner that would have the least tendency to reduce productivity in a society. For the greater the productivity in a society, the greater the possibilities of private charity to supplement that minimum. It is also difficult to comprehend how persons in need could ever be better off in a society without a guaranteed high minimum—assuming, as seems likely, that they would experience a considerable loss of self-respect once they had to depend on private charity rather than a guaranteed high minimum for the satisfaction of their basic needs.

It would seem, therefore, that persons in need would only be better off without the high minimum requirement of the Needs and Agreement Principle if persons who are productive in a society would so dislike having to contribute to such a minimum that they would choose to produce less, thus sustaining a significant loss to themselves, in order to reduce the contribution they would otherwise have to make toward providing that minimum. Yet there seems to be no reason to expect that this sort of behavior would be generally characteristic of intelligent and creative persons in society. In any case, if the previous argument is correct, it follows that persons in need would still be justified in claiming a right to the minimum required by the Needs and Agreement Principle, irrespective of what might result from their relying on private charity.

This requirement of a relatively high minimum of liberty for each person in society results from employing a particular decision procedure to determine the ways that liberty should be restricted in society. That some procedure is needed is obvious—people are constantly restricting each other's liberty in society. Neo-libertarianism combines the libertarian's moral commitment to negative liberty with a procedure that selects principles for restricting liberty on the basis of a unanimous agreement in which everyone's particular interests receive a fair hearing. In this way, neo-libertarianism justifies the Needs and Agreement Principle and the more extensive state that would be necessary to implement that principle. Given the evident moral basis for adopting this particular decision procedure, libertarians would have to abandon their moral commitment to the ideal of negative liberty to avoid endorsing the political program of neo-libertarianism. One would think that price is more than any libertarian would want to pay.

6. Abortion, Distant Peoples, and Future Generations

IN CHAPTER 2 THE basis for the rights of distant peoples and future generations was briefly discussed. In this chapter, the topic is taken up again, with special emphasis on what implications such rights have for the problem of abortion.

It would appear that those who favor a liberal view on abortion and thus tend to support "abortion on demand" are just as likely to support the rights of distant peoples to basic economic assistance and the rights of future generations to a fair share of the world's resources. Yet, as I shall argue, many of the arguments offered by those who favor a liberal view on abortion, in support of abortion on demand, are actually inconsistent with a workable defense of these other social goals. If I am right, many of those who favor a liberal view on abortion (whom I shall henceforth refer to as "liberals") will have to make an unwelcome choice: either moderate their support for abortion or moderate their commitment to the rights of distant peoples and future generations. I shall argue that the most promising way for liberals to make this choice, given that the rights of distant peoples and future generations are so firmly grounded on fundamental moral requirements, is to moderate their support for abortion.

126

The Welfare Rights of Distant Peoples

It used to be argued that the welfare rights of distant peoples would eventually be met as a "by-product" of the continued economic growth of the technologically developed nations of the world. It was believed that the transfer of investment and technology to the less-developed nations of the world would eventually, if not make everyone well off, at least satisfy everyone's basic needs. Now we are not so sure; more and more evidence points to the conclusion that without substantial sacrifice on the part of the technologically developed nations of the world, many of the less-developed nations will never be able to provide their members with even the basic necessities for survival. For example, it has been projected that in order to reduce the income gap between the technologically developed nations and the underdeveloped nations to a ratio of 5 to 1 and the income gap between the technologically developed nations and the developing nations to 3 to 1 would require a total investment of $7,200 billion (in 1963 dollars) over the next fifty years.[1] (For comparison, the Gross National Product of the United States for 1973 was about $992 billion [in 1963 dollars].) Even those who argue that an almost utopian world situation will obtain in the distant future still would have to admit that, unless the technologically developed nations adopt some policy of redistribution, malnutrition and starvation will continue in less-developed nations for many years to come.[2] Thus recognition of the welfare rights of distant peoples would appear to have significant consequences for developed and underdeveloped nations alike.

Of course, there are various senses in which distant peoples can be said to have welfare rights and various moral grounds on which those rights can be justified. First of all, the welfare rights of distant peoples can be understood to be either "action" rights or "recipient" rights. An action right is a right to act in some specified manner. For example, a constitutional right to liberty is usually understood to be an action right; it guarantees each citizen the right to act in any manner that does not unjustifiably interfere with any other citizen's constitutional rights. On the other hand, a recipient right is a right to receive specific goods or services. Typical recipient rights are the right to have a loan repaid and the right to receive one's just earnings. Secondly, the welfare rights of distant peoples can be understood to be either *in personam* rights or *in rem* rights. In personam rights are the rights that hold against some specific, nameable person or persons, while in rem rights hold against "the world at large," that is, against everyone who will ever by in a position to act upon the rights in question. The constitutional right to liberty is usually understood to be an in rem right while the right to have a loan repaid or the right to receive one's just earnings are typical in personam rights. Finally, the welfare rights of distant peoples can be understood to be either legal rights, that is, rights that *are enforced* by legal sanctions, or moral rights, that is, rights that *ought to be enforced,* either simply by moral sanctions or by both moral and legal sanctions. Accordingly, what distinguishes the moral rights of distant peoples from the requirements of supererogation (the nonfulfillment of which is never blameworthy) is that the former, but not the latter, can be justifiably enforced either by moral sanctions or by moral and legal sanctions. Since our immediate concern will be to establish the moral rights of distant peoples to a certain minimum of welfare, "right(s)" should hereafter be understood as short for "moral right(s)."

Of the various moral grounds for justifying the welfare rights of distant peoples, quite possibly the most evident are those which appeal either to a right to life or a right to fair treatment. Indeed, whether a person's right to life is interpreted as an action right or a recipient right, it is possible to show that the right justifies welfare rights that amply provide for a person's basic needs. Alternatively, it is possible to justify those same welfare rights on the basis of a person's recipient right to fair treatment.

Thus suppose that a person's right to life is a recipient right. So understood, the person's right to life would most plausibly be interpreted as a right to receive goods and services that are necessary for satisfying his basic needs, thus preserving his life in the fullest sense. For a person's basic needs are those which must be satisfied in order not to seriously endanger his health and sanity. Sometimes, of course, because others have assumed the relevant social roles or contractual obligations (e.g., the role of a parent or the obligations of a marriage partner), a person may come to have a recipient right to life that is also an in personam right, but if a person's recipient right to life is to be universal, in the sense that it is possessed by every person (as the right to life is generally understood to be), it must be an in rem right. This is because an in rem right, unlike an in personam right, does not require for its possession the assumption by other persons of any special social roles or contractual obligations. Interpreted as a recipient in rem right, therefore, a person's right to life would clearly justify the welfare rights of distant peoples to have their basic needs satisfied.

Suppose, on the other hand, that a person's right to life is an action right. Here again, if the right is to be a universal right, possessed by all persons, then it must be an in rem right. So understood, the right would justify certain actions against everyone in a position to be affected by those actions.

But what actions would this right to life justify? If one's basic needs have not been met, would a person's right to life justify his taking the goods he needs from the surplus possessions of those who already have satisfied their own basic needs? As it is standardly interpreted, a person's action right to life would not justify such actions.[3] Instead, a person's action right to life is usually understood to be limited in such circumstances by the property rights of those who have more than enough to satisfy their own basic needs. Moreover, those who claim property rights to such surplus goods are usually in a position effectively to prohibit those in need from taking what they require. For surely most underdeveloped nations of the world would be able to sponsor expeditions to the American Midwest or the Australian Plains for the purpose of collecting the grain that is necessary to satisfy the basic needs of their citizens, if they were not effectively prohibited from doing so at almost every stage of the enterprise.

But are persons with surplus goods normally justified in so prohibiting others from satisfying their basic needs? Admittedly, such persons may have contributed greatly to the value of the surplus goods they possess, but why should that give them power over the life and death of those who are less fortunate? While their contribution may well justify favoring their nonbasic needs over the nonbasic needs of others, how could it justify favoring their nonbasic needs over the basic needs of others? After all, a person's action right of life, being a universal right, does not depend on the assumption by other persons of any special social roles or contractual obligations, whereas, by contrast, a person normally acquires property rights only when *other persons* assume the relevant social roles or contractual obligations, such as the role of a neighbor or the obligation of a merchant. Consequently, it would seem that a person's action right to acquire the goods necessary to satisfy his basic needs could not be limited by the property rights of others, unless the person himself had voluntarily agreed to be so constrained by those property rights. But obviously, few people would voluntarily agree to have such constraints placed upon their ability to acquire the goods necessary to satisfy their basic needs. For most people, their right to acquire the social goods necessary to satisfy their basic needs would have priority over any other person's property rights, or, alternatively, they would conceive of property rights in such a way that no one could have property rights to any surplus goods which were required to satisfy their own basic needs.

Even if some property rights could arise, not by the assumption of any special roles or contractual obligations but by a Lockean process of mixing one's labor with previously unowned goods and resources, there would still be a need for a morally acceptable restriction on such appropriations. For otherwise *moral rights* to property would not arise. But for a restriction on such appropriations to be morally acceptable, the same sort of restriction that limits property rights, when the acceptance of the relevant social roles or contractual obligations is required, should likewise limit property rights when that acceptance is not required. This means, then, that in order to give rise to property rights without the acceptance of the relevant social roles and contractual obligations, the appropriation of previously unowned goods and resources cannot justifiably limit anyone else's ability to acquire the social goods necessary to satisfy his basic needs, unless the person could reasonably be expected to voluntarily agree to be so constrained. In fact, Locke's own restriction that "there is enough and as good left in common for others" seems to express the same sort of requirement. This means that a person's action, in rem right to life, interpreted as a right to acquire the social goods necessary to satisfy his basic needs, would be unlimited by any property rights, unless the person voluntarily agreed (or could be reasonably expected to voluntarily agree) to be so constrained. So understood, a person's action right to life would clearly justify the welfare rights of distant peoples.

If we turn to a consideration of a person's right to fair treatment, a similar justification of the welfare rights of distant peoples emerges. To determine the requirements of fair treatment, suppose we employ the decision procedure used in Chapter 5. Since by employing this decision procedure we would not be using our knowledge of which particular interests happen to be our own, we would be quite concerned about the pattern by which goods would be distributed throughout the world. By using the decision procedure, we would reason as though our particular interests might be those of persons with the smallest share of goods. This does not mean that we would want to secure the highest possible minimum for those who are least advantaged, for that would require sacrificing many of the nonbasic needs of those who in fact choose to be unproductive. Nevertheless, we would still have reason to ensure that each person had the necessary goods to satisfy his or her basic needs, irrespective of the technological development of the nation to which the person belongs. It seem clear, therefore, that a right to fair treatment, as captured by this decision procedure, would also justify the welfare right of distant peoples.

Distant Peoples and Abortion

What the preceding arguments have shown is that the welfare rights of distant peoples can be firmly grounded either in each person's right to life or in each person's right to fair treatment. As a result, it would seem impossible for one to deny that each person has a right to life or a right to fair treatment without also denying the welfare rights of distant peoples, and similarly impossible to deny that distant peoples have welfare rights without also either denying that each person has a right to life and a right to fair treatment or else drastically reinterpreting the significance of those rights. However, if one affirms the welfare rights of distant peoples, as liberals tend to do, there are certain arguments in defense of abortion that one should in consistency reject. These arguments for abortion all begin with the assumption that the fetus is a person and then attempt to show that abortion can still be justified in many cases.

One such argument is based on a distinction between what a person can demand as a right and what is required by moral decency. Abortion, it is said, may offend against the requirements of moral decency, but it rarely, if ever, violates anyone's rights. Judith Jarvis Thomson illustrates this view as follows:

> ... even supposing a case in which a woman pregnant due to rape ought to allow the unborn person to use her body for the hour he needs, we should not conclude that he has a right to do so; we should conclude that she is self-centered, callous, indecent, but not unjust if she refuses.[4]

In Thomson's example, the sacrifice the pregnant woman would have to make to save the innocent fetus-person's life is certainly quite minimal.[5] Yet Thomson and other defenders of abortion contend that this minimal sacrifice is simply a requirement of moral decency and that neither justice nor the rights of the fetus-person require the woman to contribute the use of her womb even for one hour! But if such a minimal life-sustaining sacrifice is neither required by justice nor by the rights of the fetus-person, how could one maintain that distant peoples have a right to have their basic needs satisfied? Obviously, to satisfy the basic needs of distant peoples would require a considerable sacrifice from many people in the technologically developed nations of the world. Taken individually, such sacrifices would be far greater than the sacrifice of Thomson's pregnant woman. Consequently, if the sacrifice of Thomson's pregnant woman is merely a requirement of moral decency, the far greater sacrifices that are necessary to meet the basic needs of distant peoples—if required at all—could only be requirements of moral decency. Thus liberals who want to support the welfare rights of distant peoples would in consistency have to reject this first argument for abortion.

Another argument for abortion that is also inconsistent with the welfare rights of distant peoples grants that the fetus-person has a right to life and then attempts to show that his right to life often does not entitle him to the means of survival.

Thomson again illustrates this view:

> If I am sick unto death, and the only thing that will save
> my life is the touch of Henry Fonda's cool hand on my
> fevered brow, then all the same, I have no right to be
> given the touch of Henry Fonda's cool hand on my fe-
> vered brow. It would be frightfully nice of him to fly in
> from the West Coast to provide it. It would be less nice,
> though no doubt well meant, if my friends flew out to the
> West Coast and carried Henry Fonda back with them.
> But I have no right at all against anybody that he should
> do this for me.[6]

According to Thomson, what a person's right to life explicitly
entitles him to is not the right to receive or acquire the means
of survival, but only the right not to be killed or let die unjustly.

To understand what this right not to be killed or let die
unjustly amounts to, consider the following example.

> Tom, Dick, and Gertrude are adrift on a lifeboat. Dick
> managed to bring aboard provisions that are just suffi-
> cient for his own survival. Gertrude managed to do the
> same. But Tom brought no provisions at all. So Ger-
> trude, who is by far the strongest, is faced with a choice.
> She can either kill Dick to provide Tom with the pro-
> visions he needs or she can refrain from killing Dick,
> thus letting Tom die.

Now, as Thomson understands the right not to be killed or let
die unjustly, Gertrude's killing Dick would be unjust but her
letting Tom die would not be unjust, because Dick has a
greater right to his life and provisions than either Tom or
Gertrude. Thus killing or letting one die unjustly always involves depriving a person of something to which he has a
greater right—typically, either his functioning body or property the person has which he needs to maintain his life. Consequently, a person's right to life would entitle him to his

functioning body and whatever property he has which he needs to maintain his life.

Yet Thomson's view allows that some persons may not have property rights to goods that are necessary to meet their basic needs while others may have property rights to more than enough goods to meet their basic needs. It follows that if persons with property rights to surplus goods choose not to share their surplus with anyone else, then, according to Thomson's account, they would still not be violating anyone's right to life. For although, by their decision not to share, they would be killing or letting die those who lack the means of survival, they would not be doing so unjustly, they would not be depriving anyone of his property.

Unfortunately, Thomson never explains how some persons could justifiably acquire property rights to surplus goods that would restrict others from acquiring or receiving the goods that are necessary to satisfy their basic needs, even though, as we have seen, there are morally good reasons for holding that such property rights would not be justified. And Thomson's argument for abortion depends crucially on the justification of such restrictive property rights. For otherwise the fetus-person's right to life would presumably entail a right to receive the means of survival.

It is also unclear how such restrictive property rights would be compatible with each person's right to fair treatment. Apparently, one would have to reinterpret the right to fair treatment so that it had nothing to do with receiving the necessary means of survival. A difficult task indeed.

But most importantly, accepting this defense of abortion, with its unsupported assumption of restrictive property rights, would undermine the justification for the welfare rights of distant peoples. For the same sort of rights that would restrict the fetus-person from receiving what he needs for survival would also restrict distant peoples from receiving or acquiring what they need for survival. Thus the liberal who supports the wel-

fare rights of distant peoples would have an additional reason
to reject this argument for abortion.

Nor would it do for the liberal who supports the welfare
rights of distant peoples to concede that a fetus-person's right
to life supports a right to receive or acquire what he needs for
survival but then maintain that such a right is normally overridden by a pregnant woman's right to her body. For that
would mean that bringing to term an unwanted fetus-person
normally requires a pregnant woman to sacrifice her basic
needs to some degree, and generally this would not seem to be
the case. Consequently, the liberal who supports the welfare
rights of distant peoples would generally have the same
grounds for enforcing a fetus-person's right to receive or acquire what he needs for survival as he has for enforcing the
welfare rights of distant peoples.

Of course, many liberals cannot but be unhappy with the
rejections of these arguments for abortion. For although they
would not want to give up their support for the welfare rights
of distant peoples, given that such rights appear firmly
grounded on reasonable interpretations of a right to life and a
right to fair treatment, they are still inclined to support abortion on demand.

Searching for an acceptable resolution of this conflict,
liberals might claim that what is wrong with the preceding
arguments for abortion is that both make the generous assumption that the fetus is a person. Once that assumption is dropped, liberals might claim, arguments for abortion on demand
can be constructed that are perfectly consistent with the welfare rights of distant peoples. While this line of argument
initially seems quite promising, on closer examination it turns
out that even accepting arguments for abortion on demand that
do not assume that the fetus is a person raises a problem of
consistency for the liberal. This is most clearly brought out in
connection with the liberal's support for the welfare rights of
future generations.

The Welfare Rights of Future Generations

The welfare rights of future generations appear to be just as firmly grounded as the welfare rights of distant peoples. For assuming that there will be future generations, then they, like generations presently existing, will have their basic needs that must be satisfied. And just as we are now able to take action to provide for the basic needs of distant peoples, so likewise, we are now able to take action to provide for the basic needs of future generations (e.g., through capital investment and conservation of resources). Consequently, it would seem that there are equally good grounds for providing for the basic needs of future generations as there are for providing for the basic needs of distant peoples.

But there is a problem. How can we claim that future generations *now* have rights that provision be made for their basic needs, when they don't presently exist? How is it possible for persons who don't yet exist to have rights against those who do? For example, suppose we continue to use up the earth's resources at present or even greater rates and, as a result, it turns out that the most pessimistic forecasts for the twenty-second century are realized. This means that future generations will face widespread famine, depleted resources, insufficient new technology to handle the crisis, and a drastic decline in the quality of life for nearly everyone. If this were to happen, could persons living in the twenty-second century legitimately claim that we in the twentieth century violated their rights by not restraining our consumption of the world's resources? Surely it would be odd to say that we violated their rights more than one hundred years before they existed. But what exactly is the oddness?

Is it that future generations generally have no way of claiming their rights against existing generations? While this does make the recognition and enforcement of rights much more difficult (future generations would need strong advocates in the existing generations), it does not make it impossible for there to be such rights. After all, it is quite obvious that the recognition and enforcement of the rights of distant peoples is a difficult task as well.

Or is it that we don't believe that rights can legitimately exercise their influence over long durations of time? But if we can foresee and control the effects our actions will have on the ability of future generations to satisfy their basic needs, why should we not be responsible for those same effects? And if we are responsible for them, why should future generations not have a right that we take them into account?

Perhaps what really troubles us is that future generations don't exist when their rights are said to demand action. But how else could persons have a right to benefit from the effects our actions will have in the distant future, if they did not exist just when those effects would be felt? Those who exist contemporaneously with us cannot legitimately make the same demand upon us, for they will not be around to experience those effects; only future generations can have a right that the effects our actions will have in the distant future contribute to satisfying their basic needs. Nor need we assume that in order for persons to have rights, they must exist when their rights demand action. Thus by saying that future generations have rights against existing generations we can simply mean that there are enforceable requirements upon existing generations that would benefit or prevent harm to future generations. And for the purposes of this chapter, this is how we shall interpret the claim that future generations have rights against existing generations.

As in the case of the welfare rights of distant peoples, we can justify the welfare rights of future generations by appealing either to a right to life or a right to fair treatment.

Justifying the welfare rights of future generations on the basis of a right to life presents no new problems. As we have seen, a right to life, applied to distant peoples, is a right of existing persons to receive or acquire the goods that are necessary to satisfy their basic needs. Accordingly, assuming that by "future generations" we mean "those persons who will definitely come into existence," then a right to life of future generations would be a right of persons who will definitely exist to receive or acquire the social goods that are necessary to satisfy their basic needs. Understood in this way, a right to life of future generations would justify the welfare rights of future generations for the very same reasons that a right to life of distant peoples justifies the welfare rights of distant peoples. For future generations cannot be expected to voluntarily agree to have their ability to receive or acquire the social goods necessary to satisfy their basic needs limited by the property rights of existing generations. Nor would any process for acquiring property that was not based on the expected voluntary agreement of future generations be morally acceptable if it placed limits on the ability of future generations to receive or acquire the social goods necessary to satisfy their basic needs. Thus the right to life of future generations, interpreted as an action, in rem right, would clearly justify their welfare rights to receive or acquire the social goods necessary for satisfying their basic needs.

To determine the requirements of fair treatment for future generations, suppose we adapt the decision procedure used before to determine the requirements of fair treatment for distant peoples. That procedure required that in reaching decisions we discount our knowledge of what particular interests happen to be our own. Yet discounting such knowledge would not be sufficient to guarantee a fair result for future generations unless we also discounted the knowledge that we are contemporaries, for otherwise, even without using our knowledge of what particular interests happen to be our own, we could unfairly favor existing generations over future generations. Employing this modified decision procedure, we would find it rational to ensure for each generation a minimum of goods

necessary to satisfy the basic needs of the persons who belong
to that generation. In this way, a right to fair treatment, as
captured by this decision procedure, would justify the welfare
rights of future generations.

The welfare rights of future generation are also closely
connected with the population policy of existing generations.
For example, under a population policy that places restrictions
on the size of families and requires genetic screening, some
persons will not be brought into existence who otherwise
would come into existence under a less restrictive population
policy. Thus the membership of future generations will surely
be affected by whatever population policy existing generations
adopt. Given that the size and genetic health of future generations will obviously affect their ability to provide for their
basic needs, the welfare rights of future generations would
require existing generations to adopt a population policy that
takes these factors into account.

But what population policy should existing generations
adopt? There are two policies that many philosophers have
found attractive; each policy represents a version of
utilitarianism and each has its difficulties. One policy requires
population to increase or decrease so as to produce the largest
total net utility possible. The other policy requires population
to increase or decrease so as to produce the highest average net
utility possible. The main difficulty with the policy of total
utility is that it would justify any increase in population—even
if, as a result, the lives of people were not very happy—so
long as some increase in total utility were produced. On the
other hand, the main difficulty with the policy of average
utility is that it would not allow persons to be brought into
existence—even if they would be quite happy—unless the utility of their lives were equal to or greater than the average.
Clearly what is needed is a policy that avoids both of these
difficulties.

Peter Singer has recently proposed a population policy

that is designed to do just that—a policy designed to restrict the increase of population more than the policy of total utility but less than the policy of average utility.[7] Singer's policy justifies increasing a population of M members to a population of $M + N$ members only if M of the $M + N$ members would have at least as much utility as the population of M members had initially.

At first, it might seem that Singer's population policy provides the desired compromise, for his policy does not justify every increase in population that increases total net utility, but only increases that do not provide less utility to members who are equal in number to the original population. Nor does his policy require increases in population to meet or surpass the average utility of the original population. But the success of Singer's compromise is only apparent. As Derek Parfit has shown, Singer's policy shares with the policy of total utility the same tendency to increase population in the face of continually declining average utility.[8] For consider a population with just two members: Abe and Edna. Imagine that Abe and Edna were deliberating whether to have a child, and they calculated that if they had a child

1) the utility of the child's life would be somewhat lower than the average utility of their own lives;
2) the child would have no net effect on the total utility of their own lives, taken together.

Applied to these circumstances, Singer's population policy would clearly justify bringing the child into existence. But suppose, further, that after the birth of Clyde, their first child, Abe and Edna were deliberating whether to have a second child, and they calculated that if they had a second child

1) the utility of the child's life would be somewhat lower than the utility of Clyde's life;
2) the child would have no net effect on the total utility of their own lives and Clyde's, taken together.

Given these circumstances, Singer's policy would again justify bringing this second child into existence. And if analogous circumstances obtained on each of the next ten occasions that Abe and Edna consider whether to bring additional children into existence, Singer's population policy would continue to justify adding new children, irrespective of the general decline in average utility that resulted from each new addition to Abe and Edna's family. Thus Singer's policy has the same undesirable result as the policy of total utility. It avoids the severe restriction on population increase of the policy of average utility but fails to restrict existing generations from bringing into existence persons who would not be able to enjoy even a certain minimum level of well-being.

Fortunately, a policy with the desired restrictions can be grounded on the welfare rights of future generations. As we have seen, the welfare rights of future generations require existing generations to make provision for the basic needs of future generations. As a result, existing generations have to evaluate their ability to provide for both their own basic needs and the basic needs of future generations. Since existing generations, by bringing persons into existence, would be determining the membership of future generations, they would have to evaluate whether they are able to provide for that membership. And if existing generations discover that, were population to increase beyond a certain point, they would lack sufficient resources to make the necessary provision for each person's basic needs, it would be incumbent upon them to restrict the membership of future generations so as not exceed their ability to provide for each person's basic needs. Thus if the rights of future generations are respected, the membership of future generations would never increase beyond the ability of existing generations to make the necessary provision for the basic needs of future generations. Consequently, not only are the welfare rights of future generations clearly justified on the basis of each person's right to life and each person's right to fair treatment, the welfare rights of future generations also justify a population policy that provides the desired compromise between the policies of average and total utility.

Future Generations and Abortion

Now the population policy that the welfare rights of future generations justify suggests an argument for abortion that liberals would be inclined to accept. The argument assumes that the fetus is not a person and then attempts to show that aborting the fetus is either justified or required if the fetus will develop into a person who lacks a reasonable opportunity to lead a good life. Most versions of the argument even go so far as to maintain that the person who would otherwise be brought into existence in these unfavorable circumstances has, in fact, a right *not* to be born, that is, a right to be aborted. Joel Feinberg puts the argument as follows:

> . . . if, before the child has been born, we know that the conditions for the fulfillment of his most basic interests have already been destroyed, and we permit him nevertheless to be born, we become a party to the violation of his rights.
>
> In such circumstances, therefore, a proxy for the fetus might plausibly claim on its behalf, *a right not to be born*. That right is based on his future rather than his present interests (has has no actual present interests); but of course it is not contingent on his birth because he has it before birth, from the very moment that satisfaction of his most basic future interests is rendered impossible.[9]

This argument is obviously analogous to arguments for euthanasia, for, as in arguments for euthanasia, it is the non-fulfillment of a person's basic interests that is said to provide the legitimate basis for the person's right to have his life terminated.

However, for this argument to function as part of a defense for abortion on demand, it is necessary to show that no similar justification can be given for a right to be born, and it is here that the assumption that the fetus is not a person becomes important. For if the fetus were a person and if, moreover, this fetus-person had a reasonable opportunity to lead a good life, then, it could be argued, this fetus-person would have a right to be born. Thus, proceeding from the assumption that the fetus is not a person, various arguments have been offered to show that a similar justification cannot be given for a right to be born.

One such argument bases the asymmetry on a failure of reference in the case of the fetus that would develop into a person with a reasonable opportunity for a good life. The argument can be summarized as follows:

> If I bring into existence a person who lacks a reasonable opportunity to lead a good life, there will be a person who can reproach me because I did not prevent his leading an unfortunate existence. But if I do not bring into existence a person who would have a reasonable opportunity to lead a good life, there will be no person who can reproach me for preventing his leading a fortunate existence. Hence only the person who lacks a reasonable opportunity to lead a good life can claim a right not to be born.

But notice that if I do not bring into existence a person who would lack a reasonable opportunity to lead a good life, there will be no person who can thank me for preventing his leading an unfortunate existence. And if I do bring into existence a person who has a reasonable opportunity to lead a good life, there will be a person who can thank me for not preventing his leading a fortunate existence. Thus whatever failure of reference there is, it occurs in both cases and, therefore, cannot be the basis for any asymmetry between them.

A second argument that is designed to establish the asymmetry between the two cases begins with the assumption that a person's life cannot be compared with his nonexistence unless the person already exists. This means that if one allows a fetus to develop into a person who has a reasonable opportunity to lead a good life, one does not make that person better off than if he never existed. It also means that if one allows a fetus to develop into a person who lacks a reasonable opportunity to lead a good life, one does not make that person worse off than if he never existed. But what justifies a right not to be born in the latter case? According to the argument, it is simply the fact that, unless the fetus is aborted, a person will come into existence who lacks a reasonable opportunity to lead a good life. But if this fact justifies a right not to be born, why, in the former case, would not the fact that, unless the fetus is aborted a person will come into existence who has a reasonable opportunity to lead a good life, suffice to justify a right to be born? Clearly, no reason has been given for distinguishing the cases.

Furthermore, consider the grounds for aborting a fetus that would develop into a person who lacks a reasonable opportunity to lead a good life. It is not simply that the person is sure to experience some unhappiness in his life, because in every person's life there is some unhappiness. Rather, it is because the amount of expected unhappiness in this person's life would render his life not worth living. This implies that the justification for aborting in this case is based on a comparison of the value of the person's life with the value of his nonexistence. For how else can we say the fact that a fetus would develop into a person who lacks a reasonable opportunity to lead a good life justifies our preventing the person's very existence? Consequently, this argument depends upon a denial of the very assumption with which it began, namely, that a person's life cannot be compared with his nonexistence unless that person already exists.

Nevertheless, it might still be argued that an analogous justification cannot be given for a right to be born on the grounds that there is a difference in strength between one's duty to prevent a fetus from developing into a person who lacks a reasonable opportunity to lead a good life and one's duty not to prevent a fetus from developing into a person who has a reasonable opportunity to lead a good life. For example, it might be argued that the former duty is a relatively stronger duty to prevent harm while the latter duty is a relatively weaker duty to promote well-being, and that only the relatively stronger duty justifies a correlative right—in this case, a right not to be born. But even granting that our duty to prevent harm is relatively stronger than our duty to promote well-being, in the case at issue we are dealing not just with a duty to promote well-being but with a duty to promote *basic* well-being. And as liberals who are committed to the welfare rights of future generations would be the first to admit, our duty to prevent basic harm and our duty to promote basic well-being are not that distinct from a moral point of view. From which it follows that if our duty to prevent basic harm justifies a right not to be born in the one case, then our duty to promote basic well-being would justify a right to be born in the other.

Nor will it do to reject the notion of a right to be born on the grounds that if the fetus is not a person, then the bearer of such a right, especially when we violate that right by performing an abortion, would *seem* to be a potential or possible person. For the same would hold true of the right not to be born, endorsed by liberals such as Feinberg and Narveson: the bearers of such a right, especially when we respect that right by performing an abortion, would also *seem* to be a potential or possible person. In fact, however, neither notion necessarily entails any metaphysical commitment to possible persons who "are," whether they exist or not. For to say that a person into whom a particular fetus would develop has a right not to be born is to say that there is an enforceable requirement upon certain persons, the violation of which would fundamentally harm the person who would thereby come into existence. Similarly, to say that a person into whom a particular fetus would develop has a right to be born is to say that there is an enforceable requirement upon certain persons, the respecting of which would fundamentally benefit the person who would thereby come into existence. So understood, neither the notion of a right to be born nor that of a right not to be born entails any metaphysical commitment to possible persons as bearers of rights.

Of course, recognizing a right to be born may require considerable personal sacrifice, and some people may want to reject any morality that requires such sacrifice. This option, however, is not open to liberals who are committed to the welfare rights of future generations. For such liberals are already committed to making whatever personal sacrifice is necessary to provide for the basic needs of future generations. Consequently liberals, committed to the welfare rights of future generations, cannot consistently reject a prohibition of abortion in cases that involve a right to be born simply on the grounds that it requires considerable personal sacrifice.

But there is an even more basic inconsistency in being committed both to the welfare rights of future generations and to abortion on demand. For, as we have seen, commitment to the welfare rights of future generations requires the acceptance of a population policy according to which existing generations must ensure that the membership of future generations does not exceed the ability of existing generations to provide for the basic needs of future generations. Thus for liberals who assume that the fetus is not a person, this population policy would have the same implications as the argument we considered which justifies abortion (in certain cases) on the basis of a person's right not to be born. For if existing generations violate this population policy by bringing into existence persons whose basic needs they cannot fulfill, they would also thereby be violating the right not to be born of those same persons, since such persons would not have a reasonable op-

portunity to lead a good life. But, as we have also seen, accepting this argument, which justifies abortion in certain cases on
the basis of a person's right not to be born, commits one to
accepting a parallel argument for prohibiting abortion in certain other cases on the basis of a person's right to be born.
Consequently, commitment to the population policy demanded
by the welfare rights of future generations will likewise commit
liberals to accepting this parallel argument for prohibiting
abortion in certain cases. Therefore, even assuming that the
fetus is not a person, liberals cannot consistently uphold the
welfare rights of future generations while endorsing abortion
on demand.

There remains the further question, whether liberals who
are committed to the welfare rights of distant peoples and
future generations can make a moral distinction between contraception and abortion—assuming, that is, that the fetus is not
a person. In support of such a distinction, it might be argued
that in cases where abortion is at issue, we can roughly identify the particular person into whom a fetus would develop and
ask whether that person would be fundamentally benefited or
fundamentally harmed by being brought into existence,
whereas we cannot do anything comparable in cases where
contraception is at issue. Yet while this difference *does* exist,
it does not suffice to morally distinguish abortion from contraception. For if persons do not practice contraception when
conditions are known to be suitable for bringing into existence
persons who would have a reasonable opportunity to lead a
good life, there will normally come into existence persons who
have thereby benefited. Similarly, if persons do not practice
contraception when conditions are known to be unsuitable for
bringing into existence persons who would have a reasonable
opportunity to lead a good life (e.g., when persons who would
be brought into existence would very likely have seriously
debilitating and ultimately fatal genetic defects), there will
normally come into existence persons who have thereby been

harmed. On grounds such as these, therefore, we could certainly defend a "right not to be conceived" and a "right to be conceived" which are analogous to our previously defended "right not to be born" and "right to be born." Hence it would follow that liberals who are committed to the welfare rights of distant peoples and future generations can no more consistently support "contraception on demand" than they can consistently support abortion on demand.

Needless to say, considerably more sacrifice would normally be required of existing generations to fulfill a person's right to be born or right to be conceived than would be required to fulfill a person's right not to be born or right not to be conceived. For example, fulfilling a person's right to be born may ultimately require caring for the needs of a child for many years, while fulfilling a person's right not to be born may only require an early abortion. Therefore, because of the greater sacrifice that would normally be required to fulfill a person's right to be born, that right might often be overridden in particular circumstances by the rights of existing persons to have their own basic needs satisfied. The existing persons whose welfare would have priority over a person's right to be born are not only those who would be directly involved in bringing the person into existence but also those distant persons whose welfare rights would otherwise be neglected if goods and resources were diverted to bringing additional persons into existence. This would, of course, place severe restrictions on any population increase in technologically developed nations, so long as persons in technologically underdeveloped nations still failed to have their basic needs satisfied. But for persons who are committed to the welfare rights of distant peoples as well as to the welfare rights of future generations, no other policy would be acceptable.

Obviously, these results cannot but be embarrassing for many liberals, for what has been shown is that, with or without the assumption that the fetus is a person, liberals who are committed to the welfare rights of distant peoples and future generations cannot consistently endorse abortion on demand. Thus, assuming that the welfare rights of distant peoples and future generations can be firmly grounded on a right to life and a right to fair treatment, the only morally acceptable way for liberals to avoid this inconsistency is by moderating their support for abortion on demand.

7. Conclusion

BY NOW IT SHOULD be clear that accepting an ideal of justice as fairness requires a person to make a considerable sacrifice for the sake of the basic welfare of others. In Chapter 2 it was argued that persons should make whatever sacrifice is necessary to provide a basic minimum to the members of their society. Chapter 6 explicitly extended that result to distant peoples and future generations. And similar results were obtained in Chapter 3 when this ideal of justice as fairness was applied to context of punishment, and in Chapter 5 when this ideal was used to arbitrate between conflicting restrictions of liberty.

Nevertheless, the only defense that was given for these demands was to claim that

1) such demands would be acceptable to a person who is committed to going beyond Universal Ethical Egoism by endorsing the Universalizability, Universal Acceptability, and Fairness Requirements given in Chapter 1.

2) such demands would be acceptable to persons who are morally committed either to an ideal or negative liberty (Chapter 5) or a right to life (Chapter 6).

One might wonder, however, whether resources might not exist within contemporary ethics to provide yet a stronger foundation for the demands of justice. After all, much of ethics since 1900 has been devoted to the descriptivist-prescriptivist debate over the foundations of ethics—a debate in which descriptivists have claimed that it is possible to derive evaluative conclusions from purely descriptive or factual premises, while prescriptivists have denied that this can be done. It would seem, therefore, that if a descriptivist position could be adequately defended in this debate, it would be possible to provide yet a stronger foundation for the demands of justice.

This debate over the foundations of ethics traces its origins to David Hume's view that "ought" judgments cannot be derived from "is" judgments. Thus contemporary descriptivists argue that Hume is mistaken on this score, while contemporary prescriptivists support Hume's view. Contemporary descriptivists generally attempt to defend their stance on the derivability of evaluative conclusions from purely factual premises in one of two ways. Either they argue that our ordinary use of evaluative judgments presupposes the truth of certain factual claims or they argue that at least in institutional settings there are purely factual premises which entail evaluative conclusions.

This first line of argument, however, is not at all telling against the prescriptivist. For the prescriptivist does not deny that ordinary evaluative judgments presuppose the truth of certain factual claims. For example, the prescriptivist could grant that for Archibald to say he is proud of his butterfly collection might presuppose that he worked hard at putting the collection together or that he thinks others will be impressed with the collection. But what the prescriptivist would deny is that, given that Archibald worked hard at putting his butterfly collection together, *it follows* that he is proud of his collection. Thus showing that evaluative judgments entail factual claims does little to show that purely factual claims or premises entail evaluative conclusions. And it is only this latter view which the prescriptivist rejects.

The second line of argument, however, is something with which the prescriptivist must contend. This line of argument has taken various forms, the most notable being John Searle's attempt to derive the evaluative conclusion "Jones ought to pay Smith five dollars" from certain factual premises that presuppose the institution of "promise making." According to Searle, within the institution of promise making one can derive the evaluative conclusion "Jones ought to pay Smith five dollars" from the factual claim "Jones uttered the words, 'I hereby promise to pay you, Smith, five dollars,'" together with the assumption that certain standard conditions obtained, such as that Smith was in the presence of Jones, both are speakers of English, Smith knew what he was doing, etc.

In discussing this form of argument, descriptivists and prescriptivists have disagreed whether acceptance of the derivation depends simply on recognition of the institutional rules that govern promise making (i.e., a purely factual commitment) or rather requires, in addition, acceptance of an evaluative or moral principle that endorses those rules (i.e., an evaluative commitment). For descriptivists, to say "Jones promised to pay Smith five dollars" is simply a factual claim that is deducible from other factual premises, whereas for prescriptivists it is, at least in part, an evaluative claim that is deducible from other evaluative premises.

Actually, the dispute between descriptivists and prescriptivists is even more serious, because there appears to be no consensus at all about what is to count as a purely factual premise. Some prescriptivists have even maintained that to say either that something is in someone's interest or that something is pleasant is itself an evaluative claim. But if such claims are taken to be evaluative, it is difficult to see how the descriptivist's program for justifying ethics can ever get started, because the descriptivist's derivation of ethical conclusions would ultimately have to be based on premises such as these.

Yet the failure of the descriptivist's program would not mean the failure of justification in ethics. For the evaluative premises from which an ethical theory must proceed, if the prescriptivist were correct, need not be arbitrary or difficult to

defend; they may in fact be quite basic and generally acceptable and thus serve as an adequate foundation for an ethical
theory.

Accordingly, the conception of justice developed in this
book is founded on requirements of universalizability, universal acceptability, and fairness that are quite basic and generally
acceptable. Thus while such a standard is surely evaluative,
given the difficulties with defending descriptivism and the
problems associated with the various attempts to provide a
stronger foundation for ethics discussed in Chapter 1, this
standard does not appear to be an arbitrary starting point for a
theory of justice. Of course, it may still be possible to justify
these demands of justice on the basis of still more fundamental
evaluative premises, but whether this can be done remains to
be seen.

Nevertheless, even an acceptable foundation for the demands of justice still leaves open the possibility that those
demands may be morally outweighed by other values such as
utility, human perfection, or high culture. However, now
that the demands of justice as fairness have been developed in
some detail, it should be easier to understand why such a
possibility is not a recurrent practical problem. One reason for
this is that while many traditional conceptions of justice only
take into account conditions of desert, based typically on contribution to society, justice as fairness combines considerations
of need and desert into one social ideal. Thus at least some of
the conflicts that exist between traditional conceptions of justice and other values will be resolved within the ideal of justice
as fairness itself. Another reason is that the ideal of justice as
fairness allows persons to sacrifice the rights that they are
guaranteed under the ideal for the purpose of securing for
themselves what they take to be preferred values.

In fact, there appear to be only two types of cases in
which there will be a problem of resolving conflicts between
justice as fairness and other values. In the first type of case,

there would be the possibility of imposing on a person some sacrifice of the rights that he is guaranteed under the ideal of justice as fairness for the individual's own good; that is, the imposed sacrifice would secure for the individual greater utility, human perfection, etc. In this type of case, there does seem to be a justification for violating the ideal of justice as fairness, but a strong limiting condition on such a violation would be that the person whose rights are violated would himself, without radical transformation, come to view the violation as ultimately beneficial. In the second type of case, there would also be the possibility of imposing on a person some sacrifice of the rights he is guaranteed under the ideal of justice as fairness, but in this type of case the increased utility, human perfection, etc., would accrue not to the person himself but to others. In cases of this sort, if there is to be an imposed sacrifice of a person's basic needs, even to satisfy the basic needs of others, it would seem that such a sacrifice would rarely be morally justified. But if, in cases of this sort, there is to be only an imposed sacrifice of a person's nonbasic needs, there would seem to be a greater possibility for morally justifying such a sacrifice. Yet this may only be because as we move into the area of nonbasic needs we move away from the ideal of justice as fairness to a more general requirement of fairness which can more easily be morally overridden by other values. If this is the case, then the ideal of justice as fairness itself would rarely, if ever, be morally overridden by other values.

Notes

1. Ethical Egoism and Beyond

1. See Phillippa Foot, "Morality as a System of Hypothetical Imperatives," *Philosophical Review,* 1972, pp. 305–316; William David Solomon, "Moral Reasons," *American Philosophical Quarterly,* 1975, pp. 331–339.

2. See Jesse Kalin, "Baier's Refutation of Ethical Egoism," *Philosophical Studies,* 1971, pp. 74–78.

3. Jesse Kalin, "In Defense of Egoism," in *Morality and Rational Self-Interest,* ed. David Gauthier (Englewood Cliffs, N.J., 1970), pp. 73–74.

4. In speaking of different uses of "ought" I do not want to deny that there might also be some minimal univocal sense of "ought" shared by these different uses.

5. Going into business for himself would only be "indirectly" under Herman's voluntary control if it depends on his doing something else first, for example, his taking steps to acquire sufficient financial backing.

6. Kurt Baier, "Ethical Egoism and Interpersonal Compatibility," *Philosophical Studies,* 1973, p. 364.

7. For further argument on this point, see Marcus Singer, *Generalization in Ethics* (New York, 1961), Chapter 2; Alan Gewirth, "The Non-Trivializability of Universalizability," *Australasian Journal of Philosophy,* 1969, pp. 123–131.

8. It is this difference which has mistakenly led some philosophers to think that Universal Ethical Egoism is inconsistent.

9. When this same criticism is made of Universal Ethical Egoism, there is always the implicit assumption that the Universal Ethical Egoist is also employing an interpretation of "ought" with direct action-guiding implication. But, as we have seen, the defender

of Universal Ethical Egoism can consistently reject this interpretation.

10. See Alan Gewirth, "The 'Is-Ought' Problem Resolved," *Proceedings and Addresses of the American Philosophical Association*, 1974, pp. 34–61; "Action and Rights: A Reply," *Ethics* 10 (1976), 288–293; *Reason and Morality* (Chicago, 1978).

11. Thomas Nagel, *The Possibility of Altruism* (Oxford, 1970), especially Chapters 9 to 14.

12. Nagel disagrees. He thinks that the epistemological version of solipsism is ultimately dependent on the metaphysical version. See *The Possibility of Altruism*, p. 104, note.

13. Note that if Individual Ethical Egoism is similarly interpreted to allow the interests of others to count, then the justification for the position would no longer be inconsistent.

14. There are interesting similarities here to the Prisoner's Dilemma in game theory.

15. For a related discussion, see Kurt Baier, "Moral Reasons" in *Midwest Studies in Philosophy* 3 (1978), 62–74.

2. Distributive Justice

1. John Rawls, *A Theory of Justice* (Cambridge, Mass., 1971), Chapter 3. See also his more recent article, "Fairness to Goodness," *Philosophical Review*, 1975, pp. 536–555.

2. Primary goods are goods that generally are necessary for achieving whatever goals one happens to have.

3. *A Theory of Justice*, p. 156.

4. *Ibid.*, pp. 302–303, and cf. p. 124.

5. The ignorance condition would, of course, require that we imagine ourselves to be ignorant of the total number of those in the least advantaged position.

6. John C. Harsanyi, "Can the Maximin Principle Serve as a Basis for Morality: A Critique of John Rawls' Theory," *American Political Science Review*, 1975, pp. 594–606; Richard Brandt, "Utilitarianism and the Rules of War," *Philosophy and Public Affairs*, 1972, pp. 145–165.

7. *A Theory of Justice*, pp. 22–27.

8. Bertrand de Jouvenel, *The Ethics of Redistribution* (Cambridge, 1952), pp. 54–55.

9. See *Old Age Insurance*, submitted to the Joint Economic

Committee of the Congress of the United States in December 1967, p. 186, and *Statistical Abstracts of the United States* for 1978.

10. *Statistical Abstracts,* p. 465.

11. S. I. Benn and R. S. Peters, *The Principles of Political Thought* (New York, 1959), p. 167.

12. *Statistical Abstracts,* p. 462.

13. See Bernard Gendron, *Technology and the Human Condition* (New York, 1977), pp. 222–227.

14. Of course, persons in the original position would have to set standards for both private appropriation and voluntary agreement and exchange.

15. For Rawls, saving is simply capital accumulation (pp. 284–293). This seems to be the accepted definition among economists. For example, see Amartya Sen, "On Optimizing the Rate of Saving," *Economic Journal,* 1961, pp. 479–495. I doubt, however, that Rawls would disagree with my inclusion of natural and humanistic resources under the concept of saving. Moreover, that an acceptable rate of saving represents a fair contribution from each generation also seems to be generally accepted among economists, although the state of society to be realized and maintained is usually described in terms of maximal sustainable consumption. See Edmund Phelps, *Golden Rules for Economic Growth* (New York, 1966), Chapter 1; James Tobin, "Economics as an Objective of Government Policy," *American Economic Review,* 1964, pp. 15–16.

16. They might also happen to be the first generation.

17. In a recent article, Rawls proposes to get at the Principle of Saving in yet another way. He now wants to drop the assumption that persons in the original position are at least interested in the welfare of the next generation and assume instead that persons so situated want all *previous* generations to follow whatever principle of saving they would choose. According to Rawls, the advantage of this new assumption is that it does not require any modification of his initial assumption that persons in the original position were self-interestedly motivated. See "The Basic Structure as Subject" in *Values and Morals,* ed. A. I. Goldman and J. Kim (Dordrecht, 1978), pp. 58–59.

However, it seems to me that while there is an advantage to this new assumption over the previous one, in that the new assumption, unlike the previous one, leads to the Principle of Saving, it does so, contrary to what Rawls claims, only by altering his initial motivation assumption (for how else do we account for why persons in the original position want all previous generations to follow the Principle of Saving?). Thus it seems preferable to secure the choice of the Principle of Saving, as I do in what follows, in a way that does not require an alternative in the initial motivation assumption.

3. Retributive Justice

1. Immanuel Kant, *The Philosophy of Law,* trans. W. Hastie (Edinburgh, 1887), p. 198.
2. J. D. Mabbot, "Punishment," *Mind,* 1939, pp. 152–167.
3. C. W. K. Mundle, "Punishment and Desert," *Philosophical Quarterly,* 1954, pp. 216–28.
4. H. J. McCloskey, "Utilitarian and Retributive Punishment," *Journal of Philosophy,* 1967, pp. 91–110.
5. Ted Honderich, *Punishment: The Supposed Justifications* (Baltimore, 1971), p. 148.
6. H. L. A. Hart, *Punishment and Responsibility* (Oxford, 1968).
7. For further argument, see Chapter 4, pp. 104–105.
8. For example, see Richard Brandt, *Ethical Theory* (Englewood Cliffs, N.J., 1959), pp. 415–420; Abba Lerner, *The Economics of Control* (New York, 1944), Chapter 3.
9. The nonmaximin character of the choice I claim would result is totally ignored by T. M. Reed in his criticism of my earlier version of this chapter. All of his points are directed against a maximin solution. See "On Sterba's 'Retributive Justice,'" *Political Theory,* 1978, pp. 373–376, and my response, "Contractural Retributivism Defended," *Political Theory,* 1979, pp. 417–418.
10. For a discussion of these safeguards, see Herbert L. Packer, *The Limits of the Criminal Sanction* (Stanford, 1968).
11. Claudia Card, "Retributive Penal Liability," *American Philosophical Quarterly,* Monograph Series no. 7 (1973), pp. 26–35.
12. See my paper "Can a Person Deserve Mercy?" *Journal of Social Philosophy,* 1978.
13. To the extent that the laws are not reasonably just, as determined by the representatives to the meeting of those seeking principles of distributive justice, allowances would have to be made in the legal enforcement system.

4. Opposing Views

1. R. M. Hare, *Freedom and Reason* (Oxford, 1963), p. 4.

2. Notice that Hare's account of the prescriptivity of moral judgments coincides with interpretation (II_m) in Chapter 1.

3. Hare, *Freedom and Reason,* p. 93.

4. In a recent article, Hare in effect argues that if a person *sincerely* forms a judgment that is both universalizable and prescriptive, then he or she must totally disregard the relevant probabilities. But here again Hare appears to be trying to bridge an unbridgeable gap. For why can't a person sincerely universally prescribe that, say, lenders imprison their debtors on the basis of the relevant probabilities? For Hare's argument, see "Relevance" in *Values and Morals,* ed. A. I. Goldman and J. Kim, pp. 73–90.

5. Hare, *Freedom and Reason,* p. 116.

6. *A Theory of Justice,* p. 131.

7. R. M. Hare, *Essays on Moral Concepts* (Berkeley, 1972), p. 107.

8. R. M. Hare, "Rawls' Theory of Justice," *Philosophical Quarterly,* 1973, p. 151.

9. Hare mistakenly thinks that with the knowledge persons have behind his economical veil, they would still judge that it is equally probable that they occupy each of the positions in society ("Rawls' Theory of Justice," pp. 246–247). But clearly the complete knowledge of the course of history and the present conditions of society provide persons so situated with considerable grounds for thinking that they occupy certain positions rather than others.

10. Robert Nozick, *Anarchy, State and Utopia* (New York, 1974), p. 230.

11. Experiments have some relevance here.

12. However, the person cannot give up his children's right to that minimum.

13. Nozick, *Anarchy,* pp. 213–227.

14. Milton Fisk, "History and Reason in Rawls' Moral Theory," in *Reading Rawls,* ed. Norman Daniels (New York, 1975), p. 67.

15. C. B. Macpherson, "Rawls's Models of Man and Society," *Philosophy of the Social Sciences,* 1973, p. 347.

16. Karl Marx, in *Writings of the Young Marx on Philosophy and Society,* ed. and trans. Lloyd D. Easton and Kurt M. Guddat (Garden City, N.Y., 1967), p. 281.

17. Karl Marx, *Capital* (New York, 1967), 1: 715.

18. Richard Miller, "Rawls and Marxism," *Philosophy and Public Affairs*, 1974, pp. 167–191.

5. Neo-Libertarianism

1. F. A. Hayek, *The Constitution of Liberty* (Chicago, 1960), p. 11.
2. John Hospers, *Libertarianism* (Los Angeles, 1971), p. 5.
3. *Anarchy, State and Utopia*, p. ix.
4. Gerald MacCallum, "Negative and Positive Freedom," *Philosophical Review*, 1967, pp. 312–334.
5. Hospers, *Libertarianism*, pp. 152–154.
6. W. A. Parent, "Some Recent Work on the Concept of Liberty," *American Philosophical Quarterly*, 1974, pp. 149–167.
7. C. B. Macpherson, *Democratic Theory* (Oxford, 1973), pp. 95–119.
8. This line of argument was developed by Eric Mack in response to an earlier version of this chapter. See his paper "Liberty and Justice" in *Justice and Economic Distribution*, ed. John Arthur and William Shaw (Englewood Cliffs, N.J., 1978), pp. 183–193.
9. In discounting knowledge of which particular interests happen to be their own, it is assumed that persons would also discount knowledge of with what probability they would have various particular interests in their society.
10. However, the person cannot give up his or her children's right to that minimum.
11. This principle is, of course, identical with the first two principles derived from Rawls' decision procedure in Chapter 2.

6. Abortion, Distant Peoples, and Future Generations

1. Mihajlo Mesarovic and Eduard Pestel, *Mankind at the Turning Point* (New York, 1975), Chapter 5.
2. Herman Kahn, William Brown, and Leon Martel, *The Next 200 Years* (New York, 1975), Chapter 5.
3. So interpreted, an action right to life would impose lesser moral requirements than a recipient right to life.
4. Judith Jarvis Thomson, "A Defense of Abortion," *Philosophy and Public Affairs*, 1971, p. 61.

5. Hereafter the term "fetus-person" will be used to indicate the assumption that the fetus is a person. The term "fetus" is also understood to refer to any human organism, from conception to birth.

6. Thomson, "A Defense of Abortion," p. 55.

7. Peter Singer, "A Utilitarian Population Principle," in *Ethics and Population*, ed. Michael Bayles (Cambridge, 1976), pp. 81–99.

8. Derek Parfit, "On Doing the Best for Our Children," in *Ethics and Population*, pp. 100–115.

9. Joel Feinberg, "Is There a Right to be Born?" in *Understanding Moral Philosophy*, ed. James Rachels (Encino, 1976), p. 354.

Index